T0301843

The Strategic Management of Innovation

The Strategic Management of Innovation

A Sociological and Economic Theory

Jon Sundbo

Professor of Business Administration, Innovation and Technology Development, Roskilde University, Denmark

NEW HORIZONS IN THE ECONOMICS OF INNOVATION

Edward Elgar

Cheltenham, UK • Northhampton, MA, United States

Published by
Edward Elgar Publishing Limited
Glensanda House
Montpellier Parade
Cheltenham
Glos GL50 1UA
UK

Edward Elgar Publishing, Inc.
136 West Street
Suite 202
Northampton
Massachusetts 01060
USA

A catalogue record for this book
is available from the British Library

Library of Congress Cataloguing in Publication Data
Sundbo, Jon.
    The strategic management of innovation : a sociological and economic theory / Jon Sundbo.
        p. cm. – (New horizons in the economics of innovation)
    Includes bibliographical references and index.
    1. Technological innovations–Economic aspects–Management.
    2. Technological innovations–Sociological aspects. 3.Strategic planning. I. Title. II. Series.
    HD45 .S887 2002
    658.4'012–dc21

                                                            2001053215

ISBN 1-84064-799-X

Printed and bound in Great Britain by MPG Books Ltd, Bodmin, Cornwall

Contents

Figures

Preface

This book represents a stage in a continuing body of work on innovation theory. The aim has been to understand what innovation is in contemporary firms and societies, and to develop a new theoretical understanding. Previous works have reviewed and analysed innovation theory (Sundbo 1998b), and this led to the identification of three paradigms and an empirical analysis of innovation in services (Sundbo 1998a), which provided many new perspectives. This book represents a third step. It uses the empirical results as a basis for developing the contemporary paradigm identified in the first book, but only developed at a preliminary stage there.

Many people have contributed to discussions and criticism that have improved the book. In particular I will mention Faïz Gallouj from IFRESI, Lille University, with whom I have collaborated in doing research and developing some of the models that I will draw on in this book (cf. Sundbo and Gallouj 1999, 2000). Faïz thus has taken part in developing the basis for the book, but the exposition here is my responsibility. I would also like to mention my colleagues in the research group on innovation and technology development at the Department of Social Sciences at Roskilde University and also Stan Metcalfe from PREST, University of Manchester, who has given valuable advice.

The work for this book has been part of the research project, 'Service Development, Internationalization and Development of Competencies', supported by the Danish Research Councils.

Jon Sundbo
Roskilde, May 2001.

1. Introduction

1 THE TOPIC: STRATEGIC INNOVATION THEORY

This book presents and discusses a sociology-based theory of innovation in firms called the strategic innovation theory. It concerns the management of innovation.

The sociological base is the core of this theory and its chief characteristic in relation to other contemporary innovation theories. However, the discussion will necessarily include elements from other disciplines, particularly economics and management science. The strategic innovation theory will also be related to economic theory, but it will be less abstract and less simply causally oriented than mainstream neoclassical economics.

It is an empirically founded analytical theory. This means that it is a theory of how firms actually behave, and is developed on the basis of empirical results. It is not a prescriptive model that tells firms how to achieve success. However, it is my hope that firms as well as researchers can learn something from the theory about the mechanisms of managing innovation and may thus become better managers of their own innovation processes.

Innovation is considered to be a phenomenon which is partly rational, partly an unpredictable social process.

Strategy is seen as a sociological phenomenon: a social process which on the basis of an interpretation of the environment – in particular the market – leads to an organizational goal. This means that strategy is not considered as a purely rational process of value-chain improvements, for example of the type that Porter (1980, 1985) introduced. The book deals with the complex social process of managing an innovative organization with strategy as a guideline, not with a few simple strategic models such as Porter's generic ones (which few firms follow). The reader will therefore not find in this book a few generic models of the market situation with associated prescriptions for how to behave on the market. Strategy comes from the internal forces of the firm as well as the market situation; however, the market situation is the most important factor. It has an inside-out as well as an outside-in perspective (cf. Alexander 1992; this will be discussed later). Its implementation is a social process within the firm – even in the outside-in perspective. This is the important thing and will be emphasized most in the book. This accords well with the function of the

1

modern flexible firm (Volberda 1998), which must constantly adjust its behaviour. The reader will find analyses and models of how the internal process of getting from strategy to innovation takes place in firms.

The internal processes of how the adjustment and development is carried out within the firm will primarily be in focus while analyses of different market situations will be secondary. This is in accordance with the interpretation of evolutionary theory that I will present: Successful selection factors in the environment can not be predicted. Thus the firm has to continuously follow the environmental development and adjust its strategy and innovation activities. The internal processes of doing that are the most important to study if one will understand innovation processes. However, the environmental factors are also important and will be discussed throughout the book.

Innovative organization has been considered as a rational process (the 'Management of innovation' tradition, for example, Tushman and Anderson 1997; Schumann et al. 1994; Tidd, Bessant and Pavitt 1997). It has also been considered as a complex, semi-anarchic process, for example by Burns and Stalker (1961) and Kanter (1983). The intention in this book is to unite both aspects and examine the dialectic of innovative organization.

The purpose is to find theoretical elements and relations among elements that can explain innovation. This will involve an analysis of the social and economic systems that produce innovations, not an analysis of concrete innovations, their quantity or their economic value.

The analysis presented in this book is a step forward in the development of a 'Schumpeter III' theory (after Schumpeter 1934) that can explain innovation as an organizational phenomenon, different from the entrepreneurship and research-and-development-based technology development that characterized 'Schumpeter I' and 'Schumpeter II' (cf. Phillips 1971).

2   A THEORY OF THE MODERN FIRM

The strategic innovation theory is a theory of the modern firm. The contemporary period is a post-Fordist one (cf. Lipietz 1987) and firms are flexible (cf. Volberda 1998). This means that they do not have a fixed organizational structure, neither in general nor for their innovation activities. Different activities and functions are woven together, and people have several tasks and participate in many different processes. The division of labour may not have disappeared, but it has become much more complicated. The organization is more characterized by loosely coupled networks.

Furthermore, modern firms have many relations outside the organization. These can be formal and informal; the firm as an official entity has network relations, and groups of employees (and individuals) have personal relationships which they use in their work.

Knowledge is a fundamental production factor as well as an innovative factor. However, knowledge in the modern firm has many forms. Some knowledge is formal and codified, some is tacit (cf. Nonaka and Takeuchi 1995). The provision and use of knowledge can follow formal channels such as a formal education or research system, but often it is an informal, situation-based provision combined with creative problem solution.

Information and communication technology is a general technology which is increasingly being used as a knowledge-providing technology, a production technology and a technology for developing innovations.

The theory attempts to capture all these factors.

Most firms at present are service firms, but many are still manufacturing ones. However, there is a general tendency for firms to change their nature to become both. More precisely, one can say that firms increasingly solve problems or provide functions. Car producers not only distribute cars as a commodity, they offer people a transport solution that may be distributed through car rental firms. The sale of cars is combined with services such as repairing, financing, travel and holiday information and general lifestyle. Many service firms also provide goods, as when a cleaning company provides cleaning chemicals. The boundaries between manufacturing and service are blurring, or one could say that all firms are developing towards becoming service firms in the sense that they sell problem solutions or experience; some of them also sell commodities. These perspectives are still in their infancy, but the development will probably accelerate in coming years.

The theory that will be presented in this book reflects this. It is developed from studies of service firms, but with a knowledge of general innovation theory (which has developed from studies of manufacturing firms) as the basis. Taking general, manufacturing-based innovation theory, going into services and then back to general theory again has been an inspiring experience. It has led to new ways of thinking about the innovation that service firms practise, and which one can also later find in manufacturing firms. The comparison of service and manufacturing also demonstrates that service firms often lag behind manufacturing ones in innovativeness and that they can learn something from the manufacturing way of thinking about and organizing innovation.

3   SOCIOLOGICAL INNOVATION THEORY AS A COMPLEMENT TO ECONOMIC THEORIES

This is a sociological theory of innovation which complements the economic theories of innovation (see, for example, Coombs, Saviotti and Walsh 1987; Dosi et al. 1988; Freeman and Soete 1997).

The theory concerns the innovative behaviour of firms.

It deals with a phenomenon, innovation, which is considered to be behavioural, and thus sociological. However, the result of the behaviour is economic. The theory is therefore related to the attempts to explain innovation from a more purely economic angle and also includes many elements from them. That is why I call it a complementary (and not, for example, an alternative or oppositional) theory.

Innovation is here seen as a broad phenomenon. It concerns the whole system and logic of change and development. Innovation is considered primarily as a process of change in enterprises. The strategic innovation theory starts with sociological phenomena, namely the organization and management of firms. It is a theory of action and interaction – not, for example, of psychological factors, like the entrepreneur theory, or of technological trajectories. The theory is at the micro level and deals with the behaviour of the firm. Thus the discussion emphasizes general elements of leadership, activities, attitudes, norms and so on. in the process of change. Innovation even becomes a factor in the power game that goes on in every organization.

From this point of departure innovation is seen as a *process* that has material results (such as new products or production methods – innovations) than the material results themselves. This is an approach to innovation that accords well with the classic studies of earlier sociologists who have analysed innovation, people like Everett Rogers (1995) and Burns and Stalker (1961), and with later organization and management theorists such as Kanter (1983), Pinchot (1985), Burgelman and Sayles (1986), Drucker (1985) and Nyström (1990).

There could be an advantage in combining Kanter's, Drucker's and Pinchot's firm-internal focus with the external focus – the strategic one – as expressed in marketing and strategy theory (see, for example, Kotler 1983; Porter 1980). This will be done in the book. Furthermore, the bottom-up perspective, empowerment (cf. Kanter 1983), will be combined with the top-down or management perspective. Within this framework, innovation becomes a broad organizational process in which many employees and managers participate.

In this book innovation is about social change in enterprises. The social change processes are important because they make firms grow and develop. However, the organization and management of innovation activities have economic consequences; they create development and growth in the firm in which they take place, and cumulatively at the macro level they create economic growth and social development in society.

In the spirit of Schumpeter (cf. Schumpeter 1934), the strategic innovation theory aims at explaining economic factors in terms of sociological behaviour.

Economic and social institutions in society are also considered in the theoretical discussion, but as secondary to the management process within the firms.

4 PARADIGMATIC ASPECTS OF THE THEORY

In my former analyses of innovation theory (Sundbo 1998b) and innovation behaviour in services (Sundbo 1998a), I found some elements that constitute the contours of what I called a strategic innovation theory. I want to develop these contours in this book.

In the former theoretical analyses, I identified three basic theories that currently compete for paradigmatic dominance in innovation theory:

1. The entrepreneur theory, in which the entrepreneur – a psychological factor – is the innovation determinant and innovations are made by an entrepreneur through the establishment of new firms. The theory has been further developed in the last two decades. Entrepreneurs are found inside existing organizations – the so-called 'intrapreneurs' (Pinchot 1985) who will be a category in the strategic innovation theory.

2. The technology–economic theory in which innovations are interpreted as technological innovations, and technicians and R&D activities are the producers of innovations. This paradigmatic line also includes the 'social construction of technology' approach (see, for example, Bijker, Hughes and Pinch 1987), as this also focuses on technology push. This theory too has been developed in the last two decades to include an emphasis on organizational and management factors and market pull – but still innovation is interpreted as technological innovation.

3. The strategic innovation theory – of which we can only see the contours. Within this, innovation is a process in which the whole organization is involved and the strategy is the guideline for the process, which is steered by the top management.

5 VALIDITY OF THE THEORY

Since the strategic innovation theory will be developed in this book, I ought to define the status of the other two theories mentioned above in relation to this development. In my book on innovation theory (Sundbo 1998b), I have stated that all three basic theories can be valid, but for different situations, which also means for different types of firm. I stand by this in the present book, and I will define the types of firm for which the strategic theory is valid; that is, firms in fields that are highly customer-oriented and have little scientific-trajectorial foundation (cf. Dosi 1982), for example service firms and low-tech, flexible, customer-oriented manufacturing firms. This is currently the most widespread type of firm. In these firms one can see the entrepreneur and technology–economic theories as special cases of the strategic innovation theory, which will then be the overarching explanatory model. The strategic innovation theory is less relevant to high-tech manufacturing firms and to entrepreneurial firms in the classic sense (one individual establishing a new firm).

However, one can argue that even in such firms the innovation process is increasingly determined more by speculation about market needs and long-term strategy than by simply scientific possibilities. This is demonstrated in different cases where I have studied manufacturing firms. Even newly established small firms grow and are forced to focus on market possibilities and establish a long-term strategy where the entrepreneur as individual is no longer the only innovation determinant. Thus the strategic innovation theory may increasingly apply to high-tech and classic entrepreneur firms too, and thus become of more general application.

My own empirical analyses have mainly been within the service sector, while most other studies of innovation have been in the manufacturing sector. Service innovations are at least as important as manufacturing innovations, since the service sector is very large and its importance to the economic growth of society is increasing (see, for example, Illeris 1996).

The strategic innovation theory is intended to be a general theory, valid for both sectors. This raises the question of whether that is possible – that is, is the innovation process similar in the two sectors? Empirical research has demonstrated that there are some special characteristics of service innovations which separate them from manufacturing innovations, but in general the innovation theories can be applied to the service sector (Miles et al. 1994; Gallouj 1994; Sundbo and Gallouj 2000; Haukness 1998).

This is even more the case with the latest theoretical elements, such as those included in the strategic innovation theory, the resource-based innovation theories (see, for example, Teece, Pisano and Shuen 1997, Foss 1993) and the learning theories (Hodgson 1998; Lundvall and Foray 1996). In many ways the strategic innovation theory has the same point of departure as these theories, and it has many of the same elements, but it is different from them. The strategic innovation theory emphasizes the sociological interaction system, not an economic resource system. It can complement the resource-based theory, but is different from it in some points, as will be explained later.

Furthermore, one of the conclusions of my former analysis (Sundbo 1998a) was that service and manufacturing converge in their way of creating innovations. The similarity of innovation processes in manufacturing and services becomes increasingly obvious as firms in both sectors become more like each other in terms of organizational forms and ways of organizing the production and delivery system. Both become flexible and develop modularized production with some standardization, as well as individual delivery to the customer (cf. Miles 1993; Sundbo 1994; Volberda 1998). In addition, service and goods are increasingly related and many firms are becoming simultaneous goods and service producers.

The main focus of the strategic innovation theory is on market-based activities. Innovation is primarily a phenomenon of renewal in firms and markets, but it may also be applied to activities in the public sector. These activities may not be subject to market conditions; they are nevertheless formal work activities where the employees are paid salaries and cost and user-quality issues are important. Social activities outside the formal economic sector in society (for example, in family life, people's free time, their relationships with other people, cultural and political activities etc.) are also important to people's lives and are also changed and renewed. However, they will often (but not always) be driven by factors other than economic activities, for example social values or ideologies that are not concerned with cost and have other means such as physical power for forcing changes in society. The renewal of these social activities falls outside the framework of this book.

The relationship between empirical results and abstract theorizing in this book is as follows. The strategic innovation theory is an outcome of the generalization of results from my empirical projects on innovation in services, primarily a project on the organization of innovation in services (Sundbo 1998a), plus a further development of the theory on its own abstract, logical premises. Results from studies of innovation by other researchers will also be incorporated into the basis of the theory. Everything will be underpinned by examples from empirical research, primarily investigations of innovation in services that I have been involved in over the last decade.

6 THE STRUCTURE OF THE BOOK

The analysis moves from outside the firm (the market, the environment) towards the centre (the internal organization of the firm) where it becomes more detailed and still more micro-oriented (the behaviour and interactions of individuals).

In Part I the framework of the theory is presented and its theoretical historical basis discussed. Chapter 2 presents the general basis of the theory and the definition of the phenomenon dealt with here – innovation. Chapter 3 discusses the strategic innovation theory as an evolutionary theory, and in Chapter 4 I discuss this theory in relation to economics-based innovation theories. In Chapter 5 the particular sociological basis of the theory is stated.

Part II presents the elements of the theory, from the outside in, that is, from market determination to organizational structure. Chapter 6 presents the market orientation aspect, and Chapter 7 the external driving forces. In Chapter 8 strategy is discussed as a modifying act whereby management decides how to react to the movements or possibilities of the environment. Chapter 9 states the internal elements with which management has to operate in the innovation process. Chapter 10 presents a model of internal innovative organization.

In Part III the innovation process is analysed as a social process within the firm. This part starts with an introduction to the general model of organization in Chapter 11. The next three chapters analyse the different phases of the innovation process: Chapter 12 the initialization phase, Chapter 13 the development phase and Chapter 14 the implementation phase. In Chapter 15 the innovation process is discussed as an organizational learning process.

The book ends by moving from the micro to the macro level. In Chapter 16 the consequences of the theory for our understanding of economic development in society are discussed under the heading 'The Interaction Economy'. Chapter 17 presents a model of the innovation system.

PART I

Conceptual and Analytical Framework

2. The Basis of the Theory

I will start by discussing the theoretical foundation for the theory, which also determines the definition of the innovation concept that is the core of the theory. This will add depth to the statements made in the introduction. In the last part of the chapter I discuss the empirical basis for developing the theory.

1 THE THEORY IS IN THE TRADITION OF SCHUMPETER

The strategic innovation theory is a step forward within an old theoretical tradition of seeing innovation as a fundamental explanation of social and economic change and offering an explanation that combines sociological, economic and business administration elements.

The science of economics has a tendency to make the sociological phenomena on which its theories are based very abstract, and to define them briefly and generally, as is the case for example with 'economic man', 'information' and 'competence'. In this book these sociological phenomena will be comprehensively discussed.

The works of several classical authors lie behind this work, and it stands on their shoulders as a further development of general innovation theory. Among these classical authors I can mention Gabriel Tarde (1895), Joseph Schumpeter (1911, 1939, 1943), Nathan Rosenberg (1976, 1982), Everett Rogers (1961), Richard Nelson and Sidney Winter (for example, Nelson and Winter 1982) and Christopher Freeman (1974).

The scientific precursor who has probably contributed most to the foundation of this book is Harry Nyström (1979, 1990). Several of his theoretical ideas will be included in the discussions in this book, but the analysis here will go further than Nyström's analysis and will relate the theory to the innovation theory tradition (cf. Sundbo 1998b). The book by Tidd, Bessant and Pavitt (1997) is also one of the book's theoretical precursors, since it operates at the micro (firm) level and emphasizes many of the same elements as this book. This includes strategy, and the book by Tidd, Bessant and Pavitt is in many ways in line with this strategic innovation theory, without using the concept. It includes a summary of recent empirical findings. Other attempts to develop a strategic, interactive

'Schumpeter III' perspective have also contributed to the basis of the book (for example, Gallouj 1997, Sundbo and Fuglsang 2001).

Common to all these authors is the Schumpeterian tradition, named after Joseph Schumpeter, who is generally considered the 'father of the innovation theory'. The Schumpeterian tradition has been concerned with answering the question 'What creates economic development?' The answer in the Schumpeterian tradition is 'Innovation does'. This is an underlying axiom of the whole tradition, and as such is not discussed within it.

However, the next logical question is 'What then creates the innovations?' There are several answers to that question; a situation represented by the different basic theories, and one that should be much discussed within the tradition, but is not (cf. Sundbo 1998a).

Schumpeter's first answer to the question was 'entrepreneurship'. The founders of new firms were the first to create high economic growth in the industrial economy. To create an innovation theory one must necessarily state the condition that the firm should be established on the basis of an innovation, and this has in fact often been the case, particularly at the beginning of the industrial epoch. However, entrepreneurship has had its day as the dynamo of the economy, as Schumpeter concluded in the 1930s (Schumpeter 1943). Having made this observation, he looked for the factor that had replaced entrepreneurship as the dynamic factor. He never really found that factor, but later research and theory has pointed to technology as the answer – giving us the technology–economic theory tradition, called Schumpeter II (Freeman 1974). Technological development became the main innovation factor. To that factor were related others such as science and research and development (R&D).

Even the technology–economic innovation theory is now losing its explanatory power, at least as the only explanation. Technological development is no longer the only, and may soon not be the most important, innovation determinant. Other factors such as organizational and market innovations, and processes other than technical science and R&D, are taking over. A new 'Schumpeter III' situation is setting in. The strategic innovation theory is a proposal for an explanation of innovation in this phase. It emphasizes the strategic situation of the firm and sees innovation as a sociological process.

This theory could be said to emphasize Kirzner's (1973) view of the entrepreneur rather than Schumpeter's. Schumpeter was concerned with finding the radical factor that led to 'creative destruction', and for him this was first and foremost the entrepreneur. Kirzner also deals with the entrepreneur as a type and with his function in the economic system. For Kirzner the entrepreneur is a coordinator and a decision-maker: he sees unutilized possibilities in the market and coordinates the internal resources of the firm to utilize these possibilities. He contributes to the creation of a perfect market and economic equilibrium. The strategic innovation theory is about how firms modestly find and exploit the small possibilities that imperfections in the market (such as a lack of variants of existing products) create. However, it also deals with the 'radical' and 'wild' ideas that Schumpeter talks about, and is thus a combination of Kirzner's and Schumpeter's views.

The strategic innovation theory takes a different approach from earlier innovation theory. Society changes and the behaviour and attitudes of individuals and firms change. Thus it is necessary at some points to reformulate our theoretical understanding. Social sciences do not deal, like natural sciences, with eternal truths; they can only produce theories that are valid for certain historical periods.

This attempt to develop a strategic innovation theory is also based on the tradition stemming from the social change theories of the 1960s (see,for example, LaPierre 1965, Moore 1963, Etzioni and Etzioni 1964). However, my intention is to take a less functionalistic and general approach than these theories, which were an attempt to apply the economic equilibrium approach to all social phenomena. On the other hand, my intention is not to create a complete situationistic or post-modern (cf. Lyotard 1984) theory in which no scientific laws can be stated and nothing can be predicted.

2 THE THEORY IS ALSO BASED ON THE CONTINGENCY TRADITION

The theoretical development in this book is also based on the contingency tradition within organization theory. This tradition emphasizes that the organizational structure of a firm is determined by certain conditions, among which external market conditions are the most important. However, internal factors such as technology, personnel characteristics and so on are also conditioning factors (cf. Donaldson 1996). Some authors within the tradition stress both external and internal conditions; others only external ones. There have also been different proposals concerning whether the relationship between the organizational structure and the contingency factors is deterministic, or whether the firm can influence and perhaps determine the environment (Volberda 1998).

This view of organizations and the way organizational structure is determined forms a natural basis for the strategic innovation theory. It fits with the idea that environmental factors and strategy are contingency factors in the innovation process, and that the organization of the process is conditioned by these external and some internal factors. The approach of this book is on the less deterministic side, that is, it does not consider the process as a Darwinistic selection process where the firm can do nothing (cf. the population ecology theory, Hannan and Freeman 1989). It emphasizes the interpretative strategy model and dynamic contingency theory (cf. Volberda 1998). The firm can influence the environment and its own conditions – but this is not easy. This view, however, fits the empirical results at which I have arrived (Sundbo 1998a).

The analysis here thus continues another fundamental tradition within innovation theory, namely Burns and Stalker's (1961) classic analysis of innovative organizational forms. Their analysis is a core element in the foundation of contingency theory – not to say the foundation itself (cf. Donaldson 1996). The analysis here extends Burns and Stalker's perspective. It takes a more flexible view of the organizational forms, adopts a more differentiated model for the innovation phases, and in particular introduces strategy as a way of explaining the relationships among environmental conditions, management and the innovative organizational structure.

3 THE STRATEGIC INNOVATION THEORY AND OTHER ATTEMPTS

The book takes the newest development tendencies in firms and some of the contemporary theoretical discussions and attempts to put them together in a way that provides an overall understanding of contemporary innovations. This overall understanding is what I call the strategic innovation theory.

The theory does not break completely with existing theory and I do not consider the former innovation theories to be completely wrong and invalid today. Changes in society take some time, and many of the old forms of behaviour continue to exist simultaneously with new forms as they develop. Elements from the former theories are also included in this one, which, however, attempts to find its own explanation.

However, the aim of formulating a strategic innovation theory has another point of departure from most of these former theories, namely a sociological view and an emphasis on the external – or market – situation of existing firms.

This explanation, which has been conceived of as a strategic innovation theory, complements other attempts to formulate a new, more valid, innovation theory. There has been a theoretical discussion which has emphasized various core elements such as innovation capabilities (Teece, Pisano and Shuen 1997), the resource-based view of the firm (Foss 1997; Grant 1991; Wernerfelt 1984), a learning economy (Machlup 1983; Lundvall and Foray 1996) and learning organizations (Argyris and Schön 1978; Senge 1995) in discussing economic development.

The strategic innovation theory will be discussed in relation to these other attempts in order to formulate a new innovation theory. The concepts and phenomena that these attempts consider will be related to the core factor of the strategic innovation theory: the strategic behaviour of the managers.

Within the attempts to formulate a new innovation theory there are two positions (cf. Alexander 1992; Wegloop 1996). One is the internally oriented, resource-based position (for example, Hamel and Prahalad 1994; Foss 1997), which emphasizes the assets or resources of the firm. The other is the external, strategic market-oriented position (for example, Porter 1990). I do not see any conflict between these two positions (the 'inside-out' and the 'outside-in'); they emphasize different aspects of modern innovation processes and may be considered as complementary. Both these approaches will be incorporated in the strategic innovation theory, although the external, strategic approach will carry greater weight. The strategic innovation theory thus goes against Hamel and Prahalad's theory that firms must keep to their core competencies, which means concentrating on their core resources – as Nelson and Winter (1982), for example, also claim. One may assume that in some situations the firms may successfully look strategically at their market situation and take in new elements outside their former core resources (or competencies).

Nor is this strategic innovation approach strictly competence-based, as is Hodgson's theory (Hodgson 1998), because it is not only competencies that are important. At all events one must operate with two types of competence which are equally important, namely: (1) scientific-technical competence (on which Hodgson bases his analysis); (2) interaction competence (such as interaction with customers). The latter is important in the internal innovation process because this is an organizational interaction process in which many employees and managers participate.

The notions mentioned above have been discussed in general frameworks, within general economics, as characteristics of the total economy in society and, within general theories of the firm, as characteristics of firm behaviour. Several of the theoretical developments mentioned above are involved in a reformulation of the science of economics. New paradigms such as evolutionary economics, institutional economics and others include new innovation theories. This book is not an attempt to reformulate the science of economics. It is only an attempt to formulate a theory for the innovation process in firms, and as such it combines economics, sociology and business administration (however, always with great emphasis on sociology).

The notions mentioned above have been considered within innovation theory as characteristics of technological innovation. Since this book does not emphasize technological innovations alone, but also considers non-technological (or social) innovations, these notions will be discussed within the framework of that interpretation of innovation.

4 THEORETICAL BASIS

The analysis will be based on three theoretical traditions:

1. Economic innovation theory (cf. for example Freeman and Soete 1997). The basis will be the newest versions, which emphasize the firm's resource base (for example, Teece, Pisano and Shuen 1997; Foss 1997) and learning (for example, Lundvall and Foray 1996). Entrepreneur theory (cf. Sexton and Kasarda 1992) will be a further basis.
2. Strategy theory. In particular, strategy interpreted as a sociological action parameter with an economic background will be the basis (for example, Pettigrew 1985; Mintzberg 1989).
3. Organizational theory. The organizational theories used will be the modified versions of the contingency theory where the firm organizes in reaction to its environment but also has an internal life that determines the organizational form (cf. Mintzberg 1989). Other elements to be considered are organization as a dual structure where management and personnel have a dialectical relationship – conflicting interests, but also mutual dependency (cf. Sundbo 1998a, inspired by Giddens 1984); roles in innovation processes (cf. Drucker 1985); and organizational learning (for example, Argyris and Schön 1974; Senge 1995).

5 THE INNOVATION CONCEPT

It is necessary to define innovation thoroughly so we know what we are talking about in the coming discussions. Too many analyses talk about innovation without defining it properly, and this often makes the discussion confusing or imprecise.

Innovation is the renewal of products and services and of the processes and organizations by which the products or services are produced, delivered and marketed. The definition of innovation can follow Schumpeter (1934) in saying that it is the introduction of new elements or a new combination of elements in the production or delivery of manufactured and service products.

Innovation is defined here as the process of transforming the ideas or inventions which are the point of departure into reality. This means the transformation of an invention into a market product, the implementation of an idea for new market behaviour, the conversion of new knowledge about the production process into a change in that process, and so forth. The invention or the idea is part of the innovation process, because without it there would be no innovation; but the subsequent stages are even more important. Innovation is primarily a matter of actions and decisions. This has always been the core issue in innovation theory – the process that leads from the entrepreneur's ability to stubbornly maintain his goal and struggle for it, to an emphasis on development in research and development (R&D) processes. This aspect is important in relation to some of the current discussions within innovation theory, where knowledge in particular has been singled out as the core factor in innovation processes. In the framework of this book, knowledge is only secondary; the primary factor is still action, which means decisions, actions and the fight to realize the innovative idea.

Another classic core issue in innovation theory is whether a phenomenon should be new to the world to be called an innovation, or whether it just has to be new to a country, an industry or a market or even to the individual firm. This has been differently defined in different empirical investigations, and it has been discussed in theoretical works, but rarely. In the framework of a strategic theory it would have no meaning to set up a criterion that the innovation should be new to the world. All our experience tells us that this is no criterion for finding activities that develop business and create economic growth. Imitations can develop business and can be included in the framework of the strategic innovation theory. This is not a theory of diffusion (as is for example Rogers' 1995), so it should concern original solutions to problems within firms. However, the firm does learn from other firms, for example firms in other industries. The delimitation of innovation should exclude the introduction to a firm of an element that is widespread in an industry, but include the introduction of an element if the firm is among the very first to introduce it. The argument is that the introduction will give the firm an advantage in the market, even if one or a few other firms have already introduced it.

This broad and somewhat fluid delimitation is reasonable from a practical point of view, and if the theory explains phenomena that are important in the real world; but it creates logical and methodological problems. Nevertheless, I prefer the relevance and value-for-practical-life aspect to the academic, strictly logical one, so we must try to live with this imperfection of the theory. So an innovation will be defined as something that is new to the industry in one country, in the sense that no or very few firms have introduced it before. This will include the strong Number Two (and perhaps Number Three) introducer in the theory, but will exclude the weak Number Four and Number Five. In practice, even this definition could create problems, since firms at present sometimes change from one industry to another, but at this point the delimitation is theoretically sufficient.

Innovations can be of different types. To paraphrase Schumpeter's diagram (1934 p. 66) for what he called development (cf. Sundbo 1998b, p. 13), we have:

1. Product innovation: a new product or a new service.
2. Process innovation: a new production method or process.

3. Organizational innovation: a new form of organization or management.
4. Delivery innovation: a new form of delivery or distribution.
5. Market innovation: a new form of marketing or general market behaviour, including a different relationship with the state and other parts of the public regulatory system, or other of society's organizations or specific consumers.
6. Raw material innovation: use of a new raw material.

These types of innovation result in either a new product or a new delivery system – in which case new elements will be introduced in the market and will give the firm an advantage in the competition – or increased productivity, which will lower prices and thus also create a better competition situation for the firm.

As mentioned above, in this book innovation is not only technological, but also non-technological. Thus innovations can have different characteristics. They can be:

1. Technological (physical objects).
2. Physical movements (that are not technological), for example, a new transport concept (but with no change in technology).
3. Intellectual, for example, consultancy.
4. Behavioural, for example, a new strategy for the company's market behaviour, or a newform of organization.

The two latter types are not technological innovations, at least not if we take technological in a strict sense as something that involves physical tools and the knowledge of such tools. Sometimes the expression 'social innovation' has been used for these. This emphasizes the sociological aspects of the innovations, for example that the activity is carried out by several people who need to interact. I will use this expression throughout the book.

Traditionally, service innovations have mainly been social, and manufacturing innovations mainly technological. We can however expect this to change in the future. Information and communication technology has given service firms, particularly knowledge-based service firms, an instrument for developing, storing and selling services. Besides, many service firms are developers of information and communication technology; the software industry is in fact a service industry. On the other hand manufacturing firms, as they increasingly define themselves in their strategies as 'problem-solvers', will, instead of providing commodities, introduce social innovations.

Besides this, information and communication technology increasingly functions as an instrument for developing innovations – whether technological or social. It is a knowledge-providing technology and it is a technology whereby firms can simulate innovations, including social ones (for example a new service can be tested through the internet).

6 EPISTEMOLOGICAL BASIS OF THE THEORY

This book is an exposition of the strategic innovation theory. I will refer to empirical results from my own and others' research in order to explain and argue for the theory. However, it is not a purely inductive or 'grounded' theory (cf. Glaser and Strauss 1970) where all the theoretical statements are based on empirical results. At several points the theoretical development goes beyond empirical results to develop a coherent, logical theory.

The general epistemological method in my research work involves alternating between two approaches in a kind of methodological zig-zagging. One is the deductive, abstract approach. A theory does not need to be empirically proven beforehand. It could be based on logically coherent abstract thinking, sometimes arguing from empirical examples, often on a common-sense basis, without being empirically tested. It should then be empirically proven afterwards. The other approach is the inductive, empirically grounded theory (cf. Glaser and Strauss 1970) where the theory is developed as a generalization of empirical results, often from case studies. Here the theory should be faithful to the empirical result, although the researcher may be allowed to go a little further than pure citation of results in the abstract development of the theory.

Each of these approaches has its advantages and disadvantages. The deductive approach creates logically coherent theories – if it is properly formulated; but there is no guarantee that it is correct in relation to reality, and sometimes this simply cannot be proven because the theory is too abstract and thus cannot be empirically tested. The inductive approach formulates theory that is empirically correct; but often it becomes limited in its scope and lacks coherence. The research process often shifts between the two approaches, either because the same researcher shifts from one to the other or because of a kind of division of labour where some researchers take the deductive approach and others the inductive.

In dealing with innovation theory I have started by reviewing the abstract deductive general innovation theory (cf. Sundbo 1998b) and have then done empirical studies (cf. Sundbo 1998a); I am now returning to the deductive, abstract, theoretical level to attempt to reformulate the innovation theory. The reformulation is based on the empirical results but, as I have said, goes beyond these.

This book is thus a further development of the empirical work I have done in the project 'Organization of Innovation in Services' (Sundbo 1998a) and involves a theoretical superstructure based on that work and other empirical research.

The empirical data on which I will draw come from that and two other projects on innovation in services: a European project (Service in innovation, innovation in services – SI4S) (cf. Haukness 1998; Sundbo and Gallouj 1999); and a Danish project (SIC 1999). The two latter projects were conducted by large groups of researchers. I will further draw on investigations of innovation in manufacturing and services done by others.

Data from services are thus the major empirical field of inspiration. However, it was rather a revelation to take the knowledge of innovation developed from studies of manufacturing and to apply it to services. It opened my eyes to new forms of innovation and new ways of organizing the innovation process, in turn providing a better understanding of manufacturing innovations, as well as of the way manufacturing and services are increasingly merging in products and firms.

However, as a logical effect of the epistemological zig-zag method, the strategic innovation theory developed in this book should be further empirically tested because it goes beyond the old theories, as well as the 'grounded' theory of the empirical projects mentioned.

3. Strategic Innovation as a Theory of Development

1 THEORY AND DISCUSSIONS OF SOCIAL AND ECONOMIC EVOLUTION

Innovation is a phenomenon closely related to economic development and social change. It is important that any fundamental innovation theory, including the strategic one, defines the character of this development and change. This issue will be discussed in this section.

Schumpeter, with his idea of creative destruction, may have opposed functionalistic neoclassical economic theory, but his idea of economic development did include equilibrium, either as the normal situation which is from time to time disrupted, or at least as a situation that occurs from time to time. Schumpeter's theory was not functionalistic in the strict sense that postulates that every element in a social or economic system exists because it has a function; but it was 'softly' functionalistic. The innovative periods of creative destruction have the function of cleaning up the economy: non-profitable mature elements are destroyed while new, high-profit and socially useful elements are introduced. The whole system will function better afterwards, and will be more useful in solving society's social and material problems.

Even the sociological counterpart of Schumpeter's economic theory, the social change theories of the 1960s (for example Moore 1963; LaPierre 1965; Etzioni and Etzioni 1964), were 'softly' functionalistic. Authors within that tradition had adopted the equilibrium idea from economics and attempted to create a logic that explained why the equilibrium arises and why it is necessary. 'Social change' was the concept used to characterize periods that from time to time disrupt the social equilibrium and create a new equilibrium. Neither of these classic traditions allowed for a situation of permanent change.

Innovation has recently been associated with the idea of evolution. Evolutionary economics (Andersen 1996; Nelson and Winter 1982; Metcalfe 1998) has become established as a paradigm within economics. Schumpeter's notion of economic development has been replaced by the notion of evolution, a concept taken from biology. Within the framework of evolutionism there would be room for the idea of permanent change. But this is not a core statement in evolutionary economics; the core assumption is that the development process is cyclical (Freeman 1984). The cyclical theory does not imply that there are no innovations and no development in the low-activity periods, only that the level of innovation activity is lower than in the high-activity periods. Whether these theories assume that there is any equilibrium in the low-activity periods is difficult to say, since this is not discussed much in the theories. Some recent innovation theories emphasize permanent change (see, for example, Peters and Waterman 1982; Wood 1988), but they cannot be classified as part of the evolutionary economic tradition.

The idea of evolution comes from biology, primarily from Darwin's theories, interpreted in a hard sense emphasizing 'the survival of the fittest'. Thus the species that are best qualified to live in a certain environment will survive, and the others will die. In this way development is progressing towards an increasingly higher level. However, in modern biology a 'softer' version has developed, where nature is seen as a complex system. Modern ecology has opened people's eyes to complexity – this is sometimes expressed in terms of a 'chaos' system (Prigogine and Stengers 1984). In this system each element can do something to better its position, even if its point of departure is bad. Furthermore, the development of the system is not considered to be unilinear as in the 'hard' Darwinist version. There are many ways of surviving,

Even evolutionism in the social sciences has its hard and soft versions. The hard version takes its point of departure in the Darwinist idea of the survival of the fittest. One factor or a few factors explain why some species survive – or, in the economic and social system, why some firms survive while others die. If we know the relevant selection factors, we can predict who will survive. An example of such a theory is population ecology in organizational theory (Hannan and Freeman 1989).

The soft version also says that some species, or elements of a system, will die and others will develop and grow. Explaining why, and predicting who will survive, are, however, very difficult. The system is very complex; mutations happen in the single element, new determinants arise and a change in one element can be propagated to others through a chain of reactions. We cannot predict the development of the whole system. We can study some determinants of the system, which may be single elements or relations between elements, and we can come to some conclusions about how the system can be influenced. This means, for example in the economic system, how a firm can behave to increase its chances of survival. The soft version is in accordance with the newest theories in biology. It is action-oriented and non-selective, as will be explained in the next paragraph.

The strategic innovation theory is based on soft principles, like modern biological theory. It is a theory of permanent social and economic development. This means that innovation is permanently on the agenda of firms as a possibility. It is not always the best option for the firm to innovate if it is to survive, but at some points it is necessary. Innovation is a strategic activity where the management decides at a given time whether innovations should be encouraged or suppressed. Innovation is an action-oriented phenomenon, not a selective one, as in Darwinistic biology, where the underlying assumption is that there are objective laws for selection mechanisms. Development is a fight between species – in this case, firms – to move on so that the particular species survives and perhaps grows at another's expense. The selection process can be influenced.

The evolutionary process is a game for which we can establish statistical or probabilistic laws which are valid for a period and a certain segment, but which are not deterministic in the way that neoclassical economics formulates scientific assumptions.

Since innovation is considered a game, the strategic innovation theory will be more a competition-oriented theory that sees enterprises as individuals than a theory of innovation systems in society. This does not necessarily imply that innovation systems as conceptualized in the technology–economic innovation theory (cf. Dahmén 1986; Eliasson 1989) do not exist. It means that we cannot start with these if we want to understand and influence innovation in firms and society. Furthermore, the importance of innovation systems has perhaps been somewhat exaggerated in innovation analyses. This is, at least, a logical consequence of the 'soft' evolutionary approach.

Strategy is a concept meant to express the attempt of the firm in question to out-manoeuvre the others in the evolutionary process and to grow itself. The development of a firm can be influenced by its actions. Certain types of action are more efficient than others, but which types these are can change from period to period.

The development of a firm can be cyclical, as can macroeconomic development. The individual firm will innovate more in some periods than in others. One may even assume that the innovation activities will come in batches, so that the macroeconomy will develop in cycles (cf. Freeman 1984). We may be able to predict the incidence of these cycles, as Kondratiev's (1935) research indicated, but the determinants of the underlying innovation activities may be different in different cycles.

The consequence of this view is that we should not start trying to understand economic and social development at the macro level either by formulating conditions for a functional equilibrium system or by studying innovation as an evolutionary macro phenomenon. We should start at the level of the firm by studying the attempts of firms to improve their innovation capability and to develop and control specific innovation activities. This is where strategic innovation theory starts.

How do we get to the macro level in this theory? We do so by summarizing the general results for the behaviour of firms. The actions that each firm takes to steer its innovation activities could be summarized, and the result would be the expression of how a country or another macro unit (for example, a region, an industry, the European Union) is behaving innovatively. The problem with such a summary is that the actions could vary from industry to industry or even among firm types within the same industry. Furthermore, it is not only an issue of the behaviour of the single firm, but also of the relationships among firms – other firms' reactions to the actions of one firm. This makes the evolutionary process complex – but that is the logical consequence of the strategic, action-oriented approach to innovation.

Some theories have stated that there exists a special system at the macro level (Nelson 1993; Lundvall 1992) which is more than the sum of the behaviour of the firms. There may be regional, industrial or national systems of innovation. This 'something more' could consist of a public knowledge distribution system, political interventions etc. Whether such systems exist and how they could fit into the strategic innovation theory will be discussed in the final part of the book.

Even though the understanding of innovation and economic growth in the strategic innovation theory is based on an understanding of the micro level – the behaviour of the firm – an understanding of macro-level innovation processes can also be developed. This understanding leads to a macro element of the theory which goes beyond the micro theory. The theory of the behaviour of the firm will be summarized in the last chapter of the book and the macro element of the theory will be developed on the basis of this summary.

2 THE SOCIOLOGICAL ASPECTS OF THE THEORY AND EVOLUTION

Since the strategic innovation theory has been said to emphasize the sociological aspects of the firm, it is necessary to state what this means in relation to innovation and evolution. The sociological aspects should also be related to the economic aspects.

The sociological approach and its encounter with economics in the strategic innovation theory raises issues of how firms can be considered as social groups, how this affects the interpretation of firms as economic entities and how this again influences the interpretation of the evolutionary process. I will discuss these issues in this section.

2.1 Firms as Economic Entities

The economic science of firms posits a market with the assumption that firms want to oust other firms. One resource in this struggle is innovation. This approach is fundamental to economics, even though it has been 'softened' in the modern institutional and other non-equilibrium-oriented economic traditions.

The soft approach too has a view of firms attempting to oust one another, even if the course of the struggle cannot be rationally predicted – neither the form of the struggle nor its outcome.

2.2 Firms as Social Groups

Firms are also social groups where people meet and relate to one another. The firm is a special type of group. It is organized with a particular goal which is twofold, namely: (1) to produce objects or problem solutions which society needs; and (2) to procure financial returns for the interested parties (owners, managers, employees) that they can use in other parts of their lives.

Innovation could be defined as exclusively concerning the activities of firms or formal economic activities. The understanding of innovation from this point of view involves economic theory. Evolution can be interpreted as organisms growing and ousting other organisms. In this framework the purpose of innovation for the individual firm becomes to oust other firms.

In contrast to this, innovation could be defined as social change (cf. Moore 1967; LaPiere 1965), in which case it concerns all groups in society, including firms. The understanding of innovation from this point of view involves sociological theory. In this approach firms are considered as social groups.

If we are talking about social groups, evolution becomes a matter of getting power over other groups. Evolution can also be interpreted as the process of survival in a changing environment. This may involve change (for example, innovation) in order to adapt to environmental changes, but it does not necessary mean that the organism needs to oust other organisms.

The main question is whether the groups (firms) attempt in their innovation activities simply to survive or to oust other groups (firms).

Social groups can do both. Simple survival is a normal state for social groups; they are introverted and are only oriented towards their own internal life. Ousting is an activity that characterizes: (a) groups in a situation of extremely scarce resources; and (b) special, aggressive groups that want power over others.

There are stable groups in which unprovoked innovations never or rarely happen. There are also dynamic groups with a looser system of norms and controls where innovations are normal. Such groups experience continuous change. The continuous change may happen in three ways:

Figure 3.1   Change determinants

Change determinant	Basis
Individual	Individual creativity
Inventions, technological development	Experiments, science
Organized goal-seeking	Power-seeking – broad organizational creativity

2.3 Firms as Economic and Sociological Entities

We thus have two interpretations of evolution, economic and sociological. In the first interpretation firms seek to oust one another, in the second they just seek to survive.

The strategic innovation theory is about the behaviour of the firm. Firms are both economic and sociological entities: economic, as entities seeking rational goals or profit; sociological, as organizations of people (although organizations of a special, goal-seeking kind). These two aspects can be united, and this is the intention of the strategic innovation theory.

Some firms attempt to oust others. Other firms do not seek maximal growth or to oust other firms, only survival. These firms are not very dynamic. This gives us a scale of more or less innovative firms. The degree of innovativeness at the same time expresses the degree of aggressiveness in ousting other firms – with the most innovative firms strongly attempting to do so and the less innovative firms mostly just attempting to survive without focusing on ousting others.

We can create a scale of four types of firms. It is described below, with the most evolutionarily aggressive firms at the top

1. The front-runners – proactively innovative (they want to form their environment).
2. The reactors – reactively innovative (when changes in the environment makes it necessary).
3. The quiet niche firms – moderately innovative (seeking just to maintain their niche position).
4. The conservatives – do not innovate (they believe in maintaining their position, perhaps in a monopoly or oligopoly situation).

Firms may have a life cycle with shifts between these types according to the market situation. Thus a given firm does not have the same degree of evolutionary aggressiveness in all periods.

3 RATIONAL ASPECTS OF THE STRATEGIC INNOVATION THEORY

Innovation, within the framework of the strategic innovation theory, is thus not a completely rational process, it is a process characterized by intentional rationality. On the other hand, the theory is not a chaos theory (as discussed, for example, by Stacey 1993). The firm seeks to guide the process rationally, but it will never succeed completely, because strategic innovation is a social process. It is a collective, organized process where there is management and a goal, but there is only a certain possibility of achieving the goal.

However, the rationality of the firm is not in this theory what has been termed bounded rationality (March and Simon 1958), which means one that satisfies instead of optimizing. In terms of innovation the firm is a trial-and-error mechanism. To innovate is to throw yourself into deep water, and is an insecure process. Innovation is a creative gamble with an uncertain outcome. However, the firm can attempt to grasp and systematize its own and others' experience. It can move from being a trial-and-error mechanism to become a search-and-learn mechanism, thus creating an experience-based rationality. There are limits to how close this rationality can approach absolute rationality, because there is still a strong creative element in innovation that makes it unpredictable.

Innovation as a means of developing the firm may be described using a fishing metaphor. You throw out some hooks and hope to catch a fish. Sometimes you do; sometimes you do not. You cannot say exactly what will happen, but you can gain some experience of where, when and how it is most efficient to throw out your hooks. Furthermore, the more hooks you throw out, the higher the probability of catching a fish, but also the higher the cost.

The questions for the firms are 'How close can the search-and-learn rationality come to the absolute rationality with which you can determine the result?' and 'How do we perfect the search-and-learn and the 'fish-guiding' processes?' We can attempt to control the processes – by considering each step. And this can be based on the systematization of experience.

However, the firm's goal is strategic, and therefore fluid. It is conditioned by the reaction of the environment, for example customers or competitors, and by the resources available within and outside the organization. Furthermore, the development and implementation process, the struggle to realize the innovative idea, takes place in a social system, so the process is subject to interaction processes that are not completely predictable. These factors make the innovation process less rational. The intentional element arises because the management plays the role of continuously attempting to keep the process on track to reach a certain goal and thus to make it rational – but, as mentioned before, without being able to do this completely.

4 INNOVATION AND CHANGE

The innovation concept can be used as a means to define and study the dynamics of firms and of the economy in an evolutionary framework. It is therefore important to identify and define the dynamic aspects. What is the relevant dynamic event?

In Schumpeter's theory, dynamics was about the disturbance of the normal economic equilibrium. Change was an exception. Currently society changes much faster than in Schumpeter's time. Firms have become more change-oriented, as demonstrated by the many analyses of and prescriptions for the continuously changing firm (Wood 1988) or the flexible firm (Volberda 1998). Firms make changes every day to keep up with the competition. The economy in society is moving towards a situation of dynamic change where the equilibrium situation is rare and of shorter duration. We are increasingly in a state of continuous change, where structural industrial changes, innovation and the strategic behaviour of the firm continuously change the economic structure, and the customers' preferences change fast. In addition the economy is becoming more global, which means that movements far away influence the national economy (cf. Reich 1991).

These developments create questions for the innovation concept. In Schumpeter's analyses and the traditional innovation theory innovation is a distinct event – something that is qualitatively different from everyday activities, which can be identified and delimited from other, repeated and routinized activities. Innovation does not happen very often.

But now change and development have become the normal situation for most – or at least many – firms. Many changes happen every day; they are part of the daily life of the firm, perhaps even a routine, and the individual change may form a very small part of the total volume of change activity. This is reflected in empirical and theoretical business literature. We need to change our view of the change and innovation process and thus of the general evolutionary pattern. Whereas the latter was based, in Schumpeter's and later innovation theories, on the idea of cyclical evolution, contemporary development theory, including the strategic innovation theory, must be based on the idea of rectilinear evolution. These ideas are illustrated in figure 3.2.

Figure 3.2   Evolutionary models

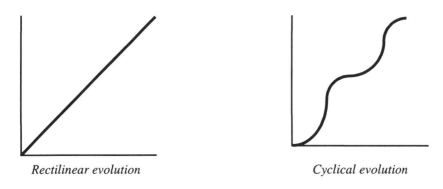

Rectilinear evolution   Cyclical evolution

This is not to say that the speed of change today is faster than in the period of industrialization in the nineteenth century that was the basis of Schumpeter's theory. It is a popular cliche, even in social sciences, to state that contemporary post-industrial society changes much faster than the old industrial society. This may be true of some elements, but not necessarily all. It may even be generally wrong. Nobody has measured it; and if they have, they have not discussed their criteria for change. The industrial revolution of the nineteenth century involved dramatic changes compared with the world that had existed for thousands of years before it. Perhaps the rate of change in every quantitatively measurable variable was not as fast as today, but the qualitative changes were great. All this means is that we do not know whether the speed of evolution has increased or decreased (nor is this really important); but the character of evolutionary development has changed – from cyclical to rectilinear.

This requires new views of the process of change and the notion of innovation. Whereas evolution once came in great leaps that destroyed the equilibrium, it now comes smoothly in a continuous stream. This is one of the main reasons for introducing the strategy concept as a core concept for understanding innovation and economic evolution. Strategy provides guidelines for identifying and steering the progression of events in a continuously changing environment (such as a war, an industry or a turbulent political situation).

One could ask 'Even if changes or innovations happen every day, might they still not follow Kondratiev's (1935) law of waves, and should the development curve above perhaps be not a straight line, but a winding one?' Yes, this may be so. However, the form of the curve is not the interesting point; the character of the process of change is. While it was formerly characterized by leaps produced by one or a few radical innovations that could be identified, it is now characterized by a constant stream of small changes in many dimensions that cannot easily be identified.

The rectilinear approach has some consequences for the concepts we use: change, innovation, development and evolution. These are the four core concepts of this discussion. They have been developed within the cyclical evolutionary approach; are they still valid or relevant? I will discuss these concepts in pairs in the following paragraphs because they are related to different levels. Evolution and development are related to the macro level, at least when we are considering macroeconomic development. Change and innovation are related to the level of the firm, or the micro level.

4.1 The Concepts of Evolution and Development

The notion of evolution has become associated with a certain current within economics which runs counter to the neoclassical mainstream. The use of the notion underlines a criticism of the neoclassical core premise of equilibrium in economics. Replacing a model of cyclical evolution with a model of rectilinear evolution should in principle not change much in this – although it may change the equations. As already stated, the purpose of this analysis is not to reform the science of economics. The use of the evolution concept might easily be interpreted as an attempt to do so, and that is one reason for avoiding the concept in the following analysis. Furthermore, the notion of evolution raises the issue of progress. It can be associated with ideas of progression towards a better society, a tendency which perhaps has its origin in some of the classic sociological and economic literature that saw industrial society as a better society where people became happier. I have no intention of making any such grandiose assumptions in the framework of the strategic innovation theory. I will postulate that many, perhaps even most, innovations solve some problems for people and help make life a little easier. However, whether people become happier as a result is an open question that I have no basis for answering. Innovations often create misfortunes. Just think of the environmental problems that thousands of industrial innovations have created. This is another reason for avoiding the evolution concept. A third reason for avoiding it is the statement that I have made earlier, namely that the strategic innovation theory concerns the survival of firms, but it is not a 'hard' theory of survival of the fittest where we can in principle predict which firms will survive. Survival is seen more as a complex struggle where each firm chooses its strategy, but where the outcome cannot be predicted simply because coincidence influences the result.

These are three good arguments for abandoning the evolution concept. One could instead use the notion of development – which Schumpeter (1934) used in his original work. This is a more neutral concept that does not have the many associations that the evolution concept has. On the other hand, it might be considered too weak in the sense that it says nothing except that things change. However, if we specify that 'development' means that qualitative changes take place – not just quantitative changes or more of the same – it can be used. The qualitative changes arise when innovations happen – when new elements are introduced or old elements are combined in a new way. With that qualification I will use the development concept throughout the book and will only use the evolution concept when I refer to the discussion within evolutionary economics.

4.2 The Concepts of Innovation and Change

Change can be a fairly distinct notion if one assumes that the normal situation is stability, as is assumed in traditional innovation theory based on Schumpeter's idea of cyclical evolution. Then change becomes something special that can be treated with its own approach and its own theory (as in the title of a now classic book *Technical change and economic theory,* by Dosi et al. 1988). However, if change is normal – everything changes continuously or at least very often – then change as a distinct notion of a specific phenomenon becomes meaningless. Change becomes everything and we cannot study everything at one time. Thus we should avoid the term 'change' within this framework. That leads us to the concept of innovation. I intend to retain the concept of innovation as the notion relevant to the phenomenon we are dealing with. There are several reasons for this. Innovation is after all an established concept within a scientific tradition, with some degree of precision and a specific meaning. The interpretation of the concept may have undergone changes throughout history, and it must be broadened and changed even more here; yet it is still a more distinct concept than change. This, however, also creates problems within this framework, which I will discuss in the following paragraphs.

Innovation has been associated with traditional innovation theory, which is based on the idea of cyclical evolution. Innovations are distinct events, different from everyday activities, and they can be studied scientifically because they can be delimited from other phenomena. Innovation is therefore a usable concept.

However, if the major condition of the survival of a business is a lot of small changes which happen every day in many dimensions, this is a different situation from the one described above. And then what use is the innovation concept? Evidently we have to work more with these concepts and discuss them in depth.

One point of departure for doing this could be the distinction that I was forced to make when studying innovation in services (Sundbo 1998a), namely that between reproduced and non-reproduced changes.

Many changes within firms are solutions to detailed problems, and the solutions will never be repeated. The traditional Fordist firm provided standard mass products produced by standard mass production methods where an innovation, whether in process or product, was always on large scale and had comprehensive consequences. Increasingly, the modern flexible firm produces individualized or modularized products (cf. Sundbo 1994), and the production process too is more flexible and can be changed to accommodate individual deliveries. These types of changes could be called non-reproduced in contrast to reproduced changes. A change is reproduced if it is repeated or introduced on large scale. If it is a product innovation, the product should be sold in many copies – like a certain model of refrigerator or a cup. If it is a process innovation or an organizational innovation, it should be introduced all over the enterprise or at least through a large part of it. If it is a market innovation, it should be introduced on large scale throughout the market. These changes are most often organized in a formal way and defined as long-term 'projects', at least at certain stages of the process.

Non-reproduced changes are only made once and on a small scale. Someone may later copy the solution if they find it in the historical files or remember it, but there is often no systematic collection of experience to draw on in order to disseminate the change. In service firms, non-reproduced changes are common. Service management and marketing theory (Grönroos 1990; Normann 1991) emphasizes the customer encounter and sees service as the ability to solve an individual customer's specific problem. Although some service production is standardized, much service is not and is a kind of 'craftsmanship'. This is the case, for example, in consultancy, advertising, garden work and construction. The service worker solves the customer's specific problem in a new way, but since other customers have other problems, the solution is never repeated. The employees create the renewal decentrally without any defined project or decision in which top management or perhaps even one's immediate superior is involved. The organization of the modern flexible firm delegates more responsibility to the individual employee, who is allowed, and even expected, to solve problems related to his work and function. This is also the case in flexible manufacturing.

4.3   The Concept of Innovation in the Strategic Innovation Theory

Is the dynamic factor – the one we are looking for when using the notion of innovation – the reproduced or the non-reproduced changes, or both? Classic innovation theory has never really discussed this question; it has taken for granted that innovations are reproduced.

Today this is a core question. It also has consequences for empirical research because the small, non-reproduced changes are heterogeneous, difficult to observe and large in number.

Here I will argue that both types of change are important to the survival and development of firms, and that consequently both must be taken into consideration (even though non-reproduced changes are extremely difficult to measure and study). I will do so by developing a taxonomy, to be described below. The changes that we are dealing with here, even though they may be small and unreproduced, are important to the survival and development of the firm. The criteria for including these small, unreproduced changes in an innovation theory is that they introduce something qualitatively new that changes the products, structures or procedures of the firm in a way that adds value.

One could argue that even unreproduced changes can and probably should be be reproduced, because they can be useful in other situations. It is only a failure in the management and organizational system that has prevented them from being reproduced. This argument is of course based on the premise that no problem (that the changes can solve), for any customer or internal to the firm's production system, is unique. I am unable to prove this point empirically, but bearing in mind the science of sociology (which has demonstrated that human beings are group animals who imitate one another's behaviour), it seems reasonable to talk of social innovations. As for technological innovations, one could argue that the traditional idea of innovation theories is that there exist unique technical problems. However, there are indications that even this is exceptional, since researchers have invented the idea of an innovation as a new combination of old technical elements, which suggests that the individual components of the problem have been seen before.

In conclusion, I will define innovation as including batches of incremental innovations and non-reproduced changes – adding that the non-reproduced changes could be reproduced to advantage. The next logical statement would then be that firms should attempt to reproduce them, and this can theoretically be conceived of in terms of the concept of organizational learning.

In a more precise determination, we could state that small, non-reproduced changes are not innovations, but that many of them are on their way to becoming innovations – they are potential innovations. They must therefore be taken into consideration if one wants to create a contemporary theory of corporate and economic development and should be included in the phenomenon discussed here (that is, innovation), although they are not yet strictly innovations. In some analyses non-reproduced changes have been defined as a particular kind of innovation – namely ad hoc innovations (Gallouj 1994).

4.4 Innovation as a Process

Innovation is a concept used internationally with two meanings: it may refer to the 'thing' – the new element or combination of elements; and it may refer to the process of renewal. Often it is not clear in theories and analyses which of these two meanings the innovation concept has. Both meanings are important – the process and the result of the process. Within the framework of the strategic innovation theory the emphasis is very much on innovation as process, on how the innovations are produced, and the research questions largely concern how this process can be improved – without forgetting the new elements themselves. The innovation concept here can be defined as characterizing a process. In the next stage the process has a certain outcome – a new product or a change in the behaviour of the firm.

5   A TAXANOMY OF INNOVATION

The different aspects of the innovation concept can be set up in a taxonomy. This separates reproduced and non-reproduced changes and places each of them on a scale.

5.1 Reproduced Changes

These are large-scale changes. They can be divided into two types, or they can be considered on a scale having two extremes:

Figure 3.3   Reproduced change

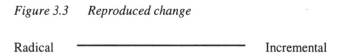

Radical   ————————————————   Incremental

This distinction was introduced by Abernathy and Utterback (1978): the radical innovations are new fundamental logics and technologies which lead to many smaller, derived innovations. An example is the steam engine, which led to the development of production machines; or the chip, which led to the IT revolution. But the innovation does not have to be a technology. The Taylorist organization of work was a radical social innovation. Incremental innovations are small, but still reproduced, changes: they are large-scale changes, but the qualitative content of the change is not very different from the earlier forms. An incremental innovation could be a new, faster version of a PC or the introduction of Business Process Reengineering as an organizational function (Hammer and Champy 1993).

The purpose of the process involving reproduced changes is to actively create a new market or new conditions on existing markets or at least to influence the market. It is Schumpeter's process of creative destruction. This proactive market creation becomes less radical as we move towards the incremental end of the scale. The incremental innovations are often market-driven (driven by the possibilities or needs of the market). If we go to the extreme radical end of the scale, the process becomes less market-driven. By this I mean that very radical innovations mostly, or perhaps always, come from the push side. Researchers or inventors invent the radical innovation as a process separate from the business processes and management of firms – for example at universities or in their own garages. However, the invention only becomes an innovation when it becomes interesting for a firm or entrepreneur to commercialize it and make a profit on it – which means reproducing it. Thus the promotion of the invention is not always driven by a wish for proactive market creation; but its implementation and reproduction is.

This is a direct development process. By that I mean that the innovation process is a systematically organized, or planned, process; otherwise the reproduction is not possible. The innovation projects are defined and can easily be found by the researcher who enters the firm. That does not mean that the process is linear – it can be very complex (cf. Kline 1985); but it does mean that the management of the firm is conscious of the process and attempts to steer it.

5.2 Non-Reproduced Changes

Non-reproduced changes are small changes. They are reactions to changes or problems in the market or internally in the firm, for example unsolved problems that customers have, or production problems that the firm has. Non-reproduced changes are expressions of a passive adaptation to market changes and internal problems. Only rarely are they part of a management strategy. Naturally they come from below, as solutions that the employees use in the 'corners' of the organization, mostly without management (at least top management) knowing about them. Thus the development of the firm through non-reproduced changes is indirect: it is not planned, no projects can be identified, and it is not a conscious act of the management or anyone else.

These changes are unsystematic, and are not organized in any way. They are outside the control of management. However, these many non-reproduced changes together move the firm and change its market position and internal organization of production. They are therefore extremely important for the firm, and it is important for management to become aware of them for several reasons. One is simply so thath managers can be aware of what is going on in the firm and where the firm is moving (it is part of management's official task to know that, but often the managers do not). Another is to be able to influence the process, either to increase the number or character of changes or to check that too many resources are not being used to create non-reproduced changes (cf. Sundbo 1996). This leads the management to want to learn how the processes of change take place and how they can be controlled, so that the non-reproduced changes can be guided by a more conscious strategy.

Non-reproduced changes are by nature isolated phenomena, but the wish to use them more systematically in a strategic framework leads to the development of a learning system (which could also develop by itself from below in the organization). The changes are included in individual and organizational learning processes. The non-reproduced changes become learning-oriented. This means that not only the content of the changes, but also the way they have been born and developed, is important. The learning process has two sides. One is learning about the process: how changes arise and how the employees' application of isolated solutions to problems could be improved (or in some cases limited). Another is the diffusion of knowledge of the solutions through the organization so that other employees who encounter similar situations can imitate the solutions.

Non-reproduced changes can also be divided into two types, which are even easier to place on a scale with two extremes, since the degree of isolation or learning-orientedness can vary:

Figure 3.4   Non-reproduced changes

Isolated   Learning-oriented

Isolated changes will not be picked up by the organizational system, but learning-oriented ones will be.

5.3 A General Model of Change

The total number of changes can be collected and expressed in a model, which places the types of change on a scale (see Figure 3.5)..

Figure 3.5   Change scale

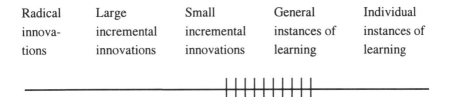

| Radical innova-tions | Large incremental innovations | Small incremental innovations | General instances of learning | Individual instances of learning |

The left end of the scale represents innovations where one radical act creates a large, sudden change in turnover or profit, while the right end represents organizational learning with many small instances which create small changes that together may change the turnover or profit. The learning process can be individual, meaning that only a few individuals in the organization have the same experience. General learning is what happens when the entire organization, or most of it, learns the same thing. The third quartile of the scale (from the left – the hatched area) is a problem, since incremental innovation and organizational learning may merge together here. This is clear from some of the new literature on innovation and organizational change (for example, Kanter, 1983; 1989), where incremental innovation processes are described as so complex and diffuse that they can be very difficult to distinguish from organizational learning processes.

In such cases, the objective phenomena are the same. The terms innovation and organizational learning therefore only represent two different theoretical perspectives that can be applied to the same phenomenon.

This is also why learning is important, because the concept covers all the small, individually based changes. These changes themselves are not learning; but learning about how employees generally get better at making such small changes develops the firm, just as reproduced changes do. Learning will be dealt with in Chapter 14.

4. Economics-based Innovation Theories and the Strategic Innovation Theory

1 THE IDEAL OF ECONOMIC-BASED INNOVATION THEORIES

Other attempts to develop a new innovation theory – a 'Schumpeter III' theory (cf. the discussion of 'Schumpeter I' and 'Schumpeter II' in Phillips 1971; Freeman 1974) have had their starting points in economics and its fundamental epistemo-logical principles. In this chapter I will discuss in detail the most important of these attempts and the innovation determinants that they identify. I will do so in order to see where the strategic innovation theory is similar to these attempts and where it differs from them.

The economics approach seeks to explain a phenomenon in terms of a limited number of factors, preferably just one – for example, transaction costs (Williamson 1975), or resources (Penrose 1959; Grant 1991). This involves an assumption of rationality in innovation theory – a single determinant of the innovation process can be found, and innovation can be explained by this determinant.

On the basis of this approach, innovation theory is developed as an abstract microeconomic theory which can be stated in a simple and logically coherent way. It becomes a theory of the firm where the details of the innovation process and the variations among different types of firm disappear. Such a theory cannot explain the innovation processes in specific firms, and remains an abstraction which focusesonly on one aspect of the creation of innovation. The theory is an attempt to find a fixed resource that can be measured and thus to place innovation in a traditional economic theoretical framework. However, the active link – *who* is doing what – is missing. The creative human being is not present, or at least not in focus, in this theory. The strategic innovation theory complements more recent economically based innovation theories because it seeks to find 'the who' – a more complicated social being than the old entrepreneur (cf. Schumpeter 1911).

Furthermore, the ideal within the economics-based epistemological approach is to make the factor in question quantitatively measurable at the macro level (for example, so that the innovation potential of a country can be measured). The macro innovation determinant should be measurable, at least in principle. It may be that we have not yet developed an instrument suitable for measuring it, but such an instrument can be developed. This has been the case with the factor that has mainly been claimed to be the determinant of innovation in the technology–economic theory (Schumpeter II), namely R&D. Researchers as well as international organizations such as the OECD and Eurostat have developed instruments for the quantitative measurement of R&D effort in different countries and industries. The same ideal is the basis of attempts to formulate a new 'Schumpeter III' innovation theory within the economic tradition.

2 INNOVATION DETERMINANTS IN ECONOMICS–BASED THEORIES

The attempts to formulate a new economics-based innovation theory propose different factors as determinants, and discussion of which factor can most adequately explain innovation currently continues. These attempts and their key factors will be briefly presented and discussed below. Most of these attempts emanate from the technology–economic tradition, but are developing outward from that paradigm. They emphasize factors others than R&D as determinants, and although innovations are still often assumed to be technological, technology does not play the same role as before.

2.1 Routines

Probably the first attempt to formulate a new theory was Nelson and Winter's Evolutionary Theory of Economic Change (1982). The authors criticize neoclassical economic growth theory and replace it with an evolutionary growth theory where firms are selected by the environment and innovation is the main selection criterion. This means that the most innovative firms will survive. As for their definition of innovation, Nelson and Winter talk about R&D and technology, without however being very explicit; but they seem to assume that innovation means technological innovation. Their innovation determinant is to be found in organizational capabilities and behaviour. They carry out no in-depth analysis of organizational structures and processes. They look for the one simple organizational factor that can be identified as the innovation determinant, and the factor they find is a structural–functional one, that is, 'routines'.

The organization of innovation is considered as a searching system – it looks for knowledge and ideas that can form the basis for innovations and market possibilities. The searching system and the ability to organize the development of innovations (what they call innovation capability) has one core factor that can explain the innovation process and the outcome of the evolutionary struggle, and that core factor is called 'routine'. It is a certain way of organizing the searching and innovation process, where this process is repeated. The routines represent the shared evolutionary memory of the firm, and have been institutionalized because these particular routines have turned out in the past to be the most efficient. The institutionalization of routines also creates a control system because employees have to follow them. This ensures that the organization functions in the most efficient way – without the manager having to check directly on every employee.

There is a learning element in the system. Routines can be changed. The firm can gain new experience that indicates that existing routines should be changed. The firm also searches outside for new knowledge. There are change-oriented routines – what the authors call heuristic routines – which search the environment to see if existing routines should be changed. For Nelson and Winter, 'strategizing' is one such routine.

Routines are thus the innovation determinant, and could be measured, or at least mathematically specified, in theoretical models. What these routines are sociologically – as processes of actions and interactions – is, however, not explained in detail in the theory.

The appearance of Nelson and Winter's evolutionary theory led to two new approaches in innovation theory. One was a view of innovation as search-and-learn systems. Learning became a core issue. The other was an emphasis on the institutional metaphor – which in general characterized the attempt to formulate an alternative economics in the 1980s and 1990s. These attempts included sociological phenomena – but only institutionalized ones – as explanations of economic outcomes. The behaviour and adherence to norms had to be repeated, long-lasting and fundamental (which is the sociological definition of an institution); continuously changing behaviour and norms cannot exhibit a single determinant that can be measured, and are therefore not suitable for an economic theory in the sense defined here.

2.2 Technological Trajectories

Technological trajectories (or paradigms) have been the determinant in some attempts to reformulate innovation theory (Dosi 1982; Perez 1983; Freeman and Perez 1988). These attempts emphasize certain routines, namely those connected with technology development. This means that there is a fundamental logical basis for a wave of technological innovations. For example, electricity has formed the basis for many small machines and transport vehicles, and microchips in combination with computer algorithms have formed the basis for the IT revolution. The logical basis and the first, radical innovation lead to other innovations based on that logic and the radical innovation.

This attempt has not left us with a view of innovation as being identical to technological innovation, but it emphasizes the process of knowledge development and learning. The remarkable thing about this theory is that it predicts that, once a trajectory has been established, it will set off a certain creative 'snowball logic' where one innovation leads to the next. If you can put a microchip in a car, you can put it in a refrigerator.

This involves great potential for incremental innovations. However, if the development of the firm follows a certain track, it also limits the firm's field of vision and prevents radical deviations from that track. The firm becomes 'path-dependent' (Dosi 1982; Teece, Pisano and Shuen 1997). Since firms can only think within the logic of the existing path, radical innovation is inhibited, among other reasons because the economic risk is too high for the management to accept a deviation from the path.

A technological trajectory may be difficult (but not necessarily impossible) to measure quantitatively; but at least it can be qualitatively identified because of its technological foundation. However, it can be difficult in practice to define what belongs to a particular trajectory and what does not. The technological trajectory remains an abstract concept.

2.3 Resources

In some literature (Wernerfelt 1984; Grant 1991) the firm is considered as a collection of resources. This approach continues with the 'routine' tradition, but in a softer version that is not as rationalistic as Nelson and Winter's (1982), and it does not assume that there is a chain of logically constituted events like the technology trajectory theory. The approach dates from Penrose (1959), who emphasized the management of the firm as an important resource for its development. In the resource-based view of the firm that has developed after Penrose, 'resource' has become a generalized concept. The firm has many resources – for example, the qualifications of its employees, its accumulated knowledge (whether formalized or tacit), its financial strength and so on. The notion of resources extends the traditional 'hard' resources of economic theory (capital, labour and land) to include 'soft' sociological resources such as management or corporate culture. Financing and physical or technical resources are also included (Barney 1991).

'Resource' has been defined as a core concept in relation to strategy (Rumelt 1984; Teece 1984; Teece, Pisano and Shuen 1997). The firm has a certain collection of resources which form the basis for its strategy. In its future development, the firm will emphasize those resources in which it is stronger than its competitors. Resources are inputs into the innovation process (Grant 1991; Christensen 1996). The firm emphasizes those resources that are strong, or perhaps those that are not strong but are necessary, in its innovation process. If for example the firm is strong in technology, it will attempt to develop technology-intensive innovations, and if it is strong in customer relations, it will attempt to develop innovations that emphasize this aspect.

The resource-based view stresses the internal resources (the 'inside-out' approach) and thus underestimates external relations – the market situation (Wegloop 1996). This idea has, for example, been the core of Porter's analyses (Porter 1980, 1985, 1990). Teece, Pisano and Shuen (1997) also classify Porter's approach as an 'outside-in' approach. The Porter view is thus viewed as the opposite of the resource-based view.

2.4 Dynamic Capabilities

The notion of capabilities has been associated with the notion of resources (Teece, Pisano and Shuen 1997). Resources have been characterized as static units: they constitute the firm's capital in a broad sense, but do not by themselves develop the firm. The theories have therefore introduced the notion of capability, which is the firm's ability to activate the resources in a dynamic way so that they can help to develop the firm and become input to innovation processes (Grant 1991; Stalk, Evans and Shulman 1992; Christensen 1996). Capabilities have been classified as either reproductive (the firm's ability to run everyday production) or dynamic (the ability to develop the firm and innovate) (Teece, Pisano and Shuen 1997). Thus the notion of dynamic capabilities is the relevant one here. Dynamic capabilities are the firm's ability to develop its resources and introduce new ones, and its ability to accumulate experience of earlier innovation processes and thus improve the innovation process.

Dynamic capabilities emphasize management and organization. They are the abilities of the managers and the organization, and may also be abilities that are not necessary in everyday work. However, in this theory the details of management and organization are not much developed because of the abstract character of the theory. Teece and Pisano (1994) mention the strategic capability of management as one element; Foss (1994) mentions management's choice between scale and scope (cf. Chandler 1990) as another.

Teece, Pisano and Shuen (1997) introduce the notion of complementary assets, which are assets that are not directly used in the innovation process, but which are necessary to the production and delivery of new products and services. An asset can be defined as a kind of passive capital (knowledge or procedures) while a capability is the activation of such capital. Innovation can destroy such assets and capabilities because they lose their importance (Schumpeter's creative destruction).

Even the notion of dynamic capability stresses firm-internal factors. However, the concept can be extended to include external factors such as the ability to absorb knowledge from outside (Christensen 1996). Foss (1994) and Teece, Pisano and Shuen (1997) discuss this issue and state that a firm has internal as well as external capabilities. The latter are abilities to link up with other firms and create relations with external actors. Foss uses this to explain how regional or national systems of innovative capabilities can develop, but it could just as easily be used to argue that the firm's competitive behaviour (not its systematic relations with other firms) are equally important. The competitive strategic view of Porter and the resource- and capability-based approaches could be combined – as is in fact the intention in this book. Internal and external factors are both important.

2.5 Knowledge

The concept of knowledge has also been introduced to increase understanding of innovation and the development of the firm. Knowledge has always been a core issue in economics (see, for example, Machlup 1983), but has lately been particularly applied to the innovation theory tradition. The interest in resources and capabilities has led to the observation that the most important of these are knowledge-intensive. Knowledge has therefore become a core explanatory factor for innovation (Nonaka and Takeuchi 1995). This has moved the focus from the action – the launching of a new product or process, or entrepreneurship – to the knowledge that forms the basis for the innovation. Knowledge can be formalized and codified, and can thus be communicated to and learned by others in a mass communication process. It can also be tacit and embedded in the minds of individuals (Winter 1987; Nonaka and Takeuchi 1995), who do not structure it in a formalized way in which it can easily be communicated to others. If other people have to learn from that knowledge, they need to have personal interactions with the person who has the knowledge.

Firms have a knowledge base which they use for their development (Winter 1987). It is a strategic asset that underlies their choice of strategy. They choose the course of development where their knowledge is most competitive compared with that of their competitors. Knowledge can even be an asset that can be outsourced to specialized knowledge service firms where it can form the basis for innovations (Quinn 1992). Thus the knowledge factor leads to a division of labour in the production system.

Knowledge is also the basis for macro innovation systems at the regional or national level (Lundvall 1988). Some authors talk about the knowledge-based economy (Drucker 1993; OECD 1996). There are coherent systems in society through which knowledge is created and diffused to firms where it becomes the basis for innovations.

The concept of knowledge easily becomes very broad and does not have to be particularly related to innovation. Knowledge is important to daily production as well, and people do have knowledge about all sorts of things, so the concept is not very closely linked with the understanding of innovation. A focus on knowledge also removes the aspect of the entrepreneurship struggle from the explanation of innovation.

2.6 Competencies

The application of the concepts of capability and knowledge to innovation theory has continued, and has led to the introduction of competencies as a concept for explaining the innovative behaviour of firms (Hamel and Prahalad 1994; Foss 1993; Hodgson 1998). Competence is the skills, abilities, knowledge and experience of the firm. Competence can be individual, but in this context it is organizational, which means that the skills, experience and so forth are characteristics of the organization and do not disappear even if individuals disappear. The notion of competence is similar to the notions of resources, capabilities and knowledge, but the theoretical discussions have attempted to make it different from these. Competence is broader than dynamic capabilities because it also includes resources; and it is broader than knowledge because it also includes the ability to activate knowledge. Even corporate culture could be included in competence (Hodgson 1998).

Competence has been discussed as a contrast to the contract, which is emphasized in transaction cost theory (Coase 1937; Williamson 1975) as an explanation of why we have firms and not only markets. Within transaction cost theory, the existence of the firm is explained by the fact that transactions are too expensive to buy on the market, so they are firm-internalized; they may be outsourced, but the providing firm will be bound by a production contract (it is obliged to maintain a certain type and level of production), and what it provides will not be a commodity that is bought on the market. Contracts are a means of obtaining control of employees and external firms. In contrast to this, the existence of firms has been explained by saying that competencies are crucial to economic development and innovation, and the firm is the place where such competencies are placed (Hodgson 1998; Foss 1993).

Some of the competencies are formalized, and some are tacit and embedded in procedures and collective corporate knowledge, which are all embedded in the firm's culture.

Competencies are the basis of innovation. The firm innovates in areas where it has competencies (for example, a certain technological area) and uses its competencies to organize the innovation process (for example, through overall corporate creativity or close relationships with and knowledge about customers).

Hamel and Prahalad (1994) have particularly emphasized the core competencies of the firm in its traditional field of production. These are strong competencies compared with those of competitors, and the firm should maintain these core competencies and use them as the basis for strategic differentiation and innovation. However, this could lead to conservatism without innovations.

Grønhaug and Nordhaug (1992) associate competencies with strategy. Competencies can be developed consciously by management; they are not gifts of nature. The management will create a strategy for the development of the firm and will include a strategy for the development of competencies, including the establishment of new ones and perhaps the abandonment of old ones. There are systematic methods for doing this.

2.7 Learning

The theoretical discussion has moved from competencies to learning. The latter is not a new concept. In 1965 Argyris analysed how learning and innovation are connected (Argyris 1965) and observed how the learning process took place in different types of firm. Learning was seen as a primarily individual process, a view that was later extended to incorporate organizational learning (Argyris and Schön 1978). Organizations can learn, and develop systems for learning which are not dependent on the individual's knowledge and learning capacity (Senge 1995).

The new aspect is that learning is now connected with economic theories of innovation and the development of the firm (Dodgson 1993) and the focus of learning is shifting from individual to organizational learning. In relation to innovation, learning is used in two ways: First, the firm can learn about its innovation process and improve its organization and management of innovation (Meyer and Roberts 1986, Sundbo 1998a). Second, learning about the input elements in the innovation process (materials, inventions, customer needs, new ways of organizing the production process and so on.) can produce new innovations (Teece et al. 1994; Hodgson 1998). The learning process is related to corporate culture (Hodgson 1998) and it is a central task for the management to manage the learning process (Dodgson 1993).

The concept of learning is even more process-oriented than the concept of competence. The latter stresses the ability to activate experience – as does the concept of capability. The concepts of resources and knowledge place more emphasis on stored experience. Learning is a step further in this process. It stresses stored knowledge as well as the process that led to the storing, and it also stresses ways of activating the experience. Furthermore, it introduces a feedback mechanism where all these procedures are changed. While competence may be measured at a given time, learning, in particular organizational learning, is so complex and many-faceted that it is hard to measure, particularly quantitatively, but also qualitatively. Organizational learning becomes part of the complex organizational development process.

The concept of learning has also been applied to macroeconomics and macro innovation theory (Lundvall and Foray 1996). This point of view is a further development of the knowledge approach. Actors in the economic system not only receive passive knowledge, but they also learn which knowledge is best in which situations, how to behave in different situations and so on. The learning aspect is dynamic, so no knowledge or behavioural routine lasts for ever, or even for a long time. Firms learn new and more efficient ways of selecting knowledge and behaviour. This makes the economic system more efficient.

The concept of learning has a tendency to become abstract, particularly in the macroeconomic version. It is also very difficult to measure learning at the macro level, because it is a complex phenomenon.

3 THE STRATEGIC INNOVATION THEORY IN RELATION TO ECONOMICS-BASED INNOVATION THEORIES

The sociological approach of the strategic innovation theory leads to epistemological ideals than differ from those of the economics–based theory. The strategic innovation theory will be more complex than economics–based attempts; it emphasizes human behaviour and sees the human being as a creative actor who can change structures and individually create innovations.

The entrepreneur theory tradition (Schumpeter 1934) has also presented a sociological, action-oriented theory. This has its economic side, just as the strategic innovation theory will have. On the other hand has the attempt to formulate a new innovation theory on an economics basis ('Schumpeter III') also has some sociological elements. Thus it is not a question of pure sociological versus pure economic theory – all the theories are to some degree cross-disciplinary – but a question of the main focus and the epistemological tradition which forms the basis.

The entrepreneur theory in general lacks the interaction aspect: the entrepreneur is a 'lone cowboy' and the focus is psychologically on his personality. It is therefore not currently realistic, since most innovation activities at present take place within organizations where people need to interact. Only a few authors have formulated theories of entrepreneurs in networks (for example Johannisson 1988). There are also theories of corporate entrepreneurship, or intrapreneurship (Pinchot 1985;Kanter 1983;Strategic Management Journal 1990), but they will be included in the strategic innovation theory.

The innovation determinants discussed by the economics-based attempts will be included in the discussion of the strategic innovation theory, but they will be combined with organizational and managerial factors.

Each of the two approaches – the economically and the sociologically based – has its advantages, and the two are complementary in understanding modern innovation processes. However, I have found that the economics-based approach becomes too abstract and too simplistic to formulate an adequate innovation theory. Furthermore, the strategic innovation theory has a foundation that is more social – based on action and interaction. Although laws can be stated for innovations, they are only probabilistic, because the theory is based on an active view of the actor: the actors in the system can change structures and tendencies. They are creative people who act contrary to conventional behaviour and wisdom. This is the ontological assumption known from entrepreneur theory ('Schumpeter I', Schumpeter 1934; Seton and Kasarda 1992). The economics-based attempts have a structural approach. They want to find the structural variables and make laws for them. These economics-based theories also have a secondary purpose besides explaining innovation, namely to reform economic theory – something that I have already stated is not the mission of this book.

However, the strategic innovation theory will not be a pure actor or process theory. It should be based on the principle that more permanent structures, functions and behavioural patterns exist, but that actors will frequently break the structural laws. The theory is in between the rational–functional, deterministic type of theory and the totally actor-oriented, non-deterministic type.

The strategic innovation theory has thus both been developed within the tradition of the contemporary innovation theories described above, and breaks with it. It is within the tradition in the sense that it is based on the same attempt to find a new explanation that emphasizes knowledge, competencies and learning, and these notions will be included in the theory. It breaks with the tradition in that it emphasizes sociological processes in the organization, and in that manaement is the point of departure for explaining innovation. In addition it is less rationalistically oriented – even though the economic innovation theory tradition is less rationalistic than neoclassical economic theory. Finally, the strategic innovation theory may differ in emphasizing social innovations (for example, organizational innovations, new non-technological services) as well as technological innovation. It is not clear whether the economics-based tradition still only deals only with technological innovation or whether it has broadened out to include social innovations. The issue is not much discussed in the literature.

The strategic innovation theory is thus complementary to the new resource–competence–learning economic tradition. It is the concrete version of what could be called the new innovation theory ('Schumpeter III'). It stresses innovation factors as they are expressed in the daily life of firms. These sociological factors, I will state, are more important if we want to understand innovation at the micro or firm level than the abstract economic approach and concepts. The latter may be more adequate to the understanding of innovation at the macro or societal level, but even there the sociological aspects are important and can be a supplement to the economic aspects.

The strategic innovation theory is different from institutional economics. The idea of strategic innovation is that it views economic development as also determined by creativity and entrepreneurship, which produce unpredictable changes. The development of the firm and economic development cannot be understood purely in terms of institutionalized norms and behaviour. Creativity and entrepreneurship do not follow a fixed pattern and are not the same in different situations in different firms. This also means that the concept of routine (cf. Nelson and Winter 1982) is not adequate to explain innovation, because it excludes the 'naughty' breaking of rules by the entrepreneur. This has also been the conclusion of my investigation of the innovation process in services (Sundbo 1998a). There are not many routines in that process; innovations are developed either coincidentally or through entrepreneurship. However, even within this framework it will be assumed that routines exist in firms; but other factors are also involved in the innovation process and are even more important than routines.

5.   The Sociological Basis of the Strategic Innovation Theory

In this chapter I will present the basis for the analysis, which is primarily sociological, and the core concepts: strategy, action and interaction. These concepts characterize the innovation process and it is through them that I will develop the theory. It is therefore necessary to discuss and define them to begin the analysis. This will lead to the formulation of the theory.

1 THE SOCIOLOGICAL BASIS OF THE ANALYSIS

This analysis deals with innovation as a sociological process. Innovation is a matter of action and interaction. This reflects what we know from studies of modern flexible firms, service firms and other phenomena that point to the importance of the involvement of employees, the interaction among employees and between the employees and customers, and independent action by employees (cf. also Kanter 1983; Bevort, Sundbo, Pedersen, 1992). These are important phenomena in production, not least when quality is emphasized, and in delivery, particularly in services where front-line personnel meet the customers (for example, Grönroos 1990; Mattsson 1993). This is also important in innovation processes.

The strategic innovation theory is based on the knowledge and theoretical generalizations we have from knowledge- and learning-based economic analyses (for example, Foss 1993; Lundvall and Foray 1996; Teece, Pisano and Shuen 1997). However, it develops these generalizations by adding interaction and action aspects, the latter from entrepreneur theory, which makes action, not knowledge, the most important factor. Knowledge and learning must be understood as a special category of the fundamental phenomenon of action and interaction. These concepts and the way the organization of innovation works must be developed first and then the importance of knowledge and learning can be introduced. This will be the order observed in the book.

The fundamental sociological approach that I attempt to establish here is neither the functionalistic approach of the social change theories of the 1960s, nor the loose, actor-oriented approach of the chaos or post-modern approach, as already mentioned. It is the middle position of mutual reciprocity: it sees social structure as determined by individual actions and values, and individual behaviour as determined by structure. Social science cannot make universal predictive laws, but it is possible to establish some general models that can explain, and therefore predict, social behaviour in specified areas, at least for a period.

This general approach to social life was probably best expressed by Anthony Giddens (1984) in his structuration theory. Giddens also operates with strategy as a core concept in understanding social behaviour. His concept of strategy described the individual's action at the micro level as the individual's way of attempting to operate in environments which are constituted by the existing social structure. This, however, can be influenced by the actions that an individual takes outside the routine or to break the routine. In the analysis in this book, strategy is seen as a more collective phenomenon, as the action guidelines for an organization. Nevertheless Giddens' approach and analysis can be an inspiration, and some elements can also be transferred directly to the strategic innovation theory. The Giddens-inspired element is further combined with the strategy concept as used in business literature, where strategy is a certain way for a firm to improve its market situation. The market situation is both the point of departure for and the goal of the innovation process, but in between the process is guided by management's attempt to reach innovative goals within the social structure constituted by the organization of the firm and related external actors. The strategy concept here becomes much like that of Pettigrew (1985), who sees strategy as a kind of organizational political process.

Organizations, which are in focus in this theoretical discussion, are interpreted in the same way. They are considered as entities which are determined by the environment as reflected in contingency theory (Lawrence and Lorsch 1967), but they can also influence the environment and therefore their own contingencies as reflected in more rational strategy theories such as Porter's (1980, 1985). Mintzberg's (1979) approach of creating different models of the contingency outcome has been an inspiration, although the analysis here is a little more on the deterministic side: believing that it is possible to find a few different variants of innovative organizations – and that one does not necessarily need to end up with as many as Mintzberg finally does (cf. Mintzberg 1989).

The view of organizations can also be said to be a combination of the rational, natural and open aspects of Scott's theory (Scott 1992).

One type of action and interaction that is central to this analysis is the decisions and actions of management and the interaction between top managers and employees. The top managers are considered to be the people who have responsibility for making final decisions and making the firm cohere. In this theory this type of action and interaction is understood by using the strategy concept.

2 THE CONCEPT OF STRATEGY

Strategy is the core concept in the theory, as indicated by its name. It constitutes the overall framework for innovation activities, and it delimits this theory from other contemporary attempts to understand innovation and economic development.

It is also important to repeat that strategy in this analysis is interpreted as a sociological concept: it concerns decisions, actions and interactions. This means that norms, values, behavioural patterns and other sociological phenomena influence the innovation process, although innovation is a social process within economic life and is therefore goal-oriented (cf. the discussion in the preceding chapters).

Strategy is thus a dynamic phenomenon which can always be the subject of interest struggles and firm-internal politics.

2.1 Many Approaches and Definitions

Strategy has been a popular concept in business literature for the last two decades, and has therefore been assigned many meanings and definitions.

In general, strategy means conscious, defined behaviour towards the market with the purpose of putting the firm in a specific future market situation. Strategy has been defined as a rational concept – a pure management instrument which characterizes a rational top-down planning process (Ackoff 1981; Ansoff 1965; 1988; Porter 1980, 1985). It has also been defined as coming from below in the organization. It has been discussed whether management really has any control of strategy (Mintzberg and McHughes 1985; Stacey 1993). However, I will state that there are at least some management aspects in strategy, in the sense that there must be some decision-making about the selection of goals and the means of achieving them.

Some analyses have emphasized the result, others the process of formulating a strategy (cf. Mintzberg 1994). Strategy has been defined as a collective process where different parts of the organization and individuals within it participate in a process of formulating and maintaining a strategy; in this case the strategy is non-rational and is not a planned activity (Mintzberg and Waters 1982). Strategy has also been interpreted as management policy (Pettigrew 1985) and this has been criticized as a mechanism for repressing employees (Knights and Morgan 1995).

Mintzberg (1994, see also Mintzberg and Waters 1982) has pointed out that the realized strategy is not necessarily the same as the intentional one, because people in the organization change their attitudes and actions, so that the real strategy changes, and the environment changes too.

The strategy concept was launched as a rational planning concept and has later developed towards a more anarchic interpretation. However, if general goal-seeking and market orientation are not retained as core characteristics of strategy, the concept loses its meaning and becomes no more than a synonym for management.

Here I will not review all the discussions and aspects – I have done this elsewhere (Sundbo 1998a) – but will go straight to the discussion of the definition of strategy and the approach I will use as the basis for the strategic innovation theory.

2.2 The Approach Used Here

Strategy is an action-related concept, designating situations where action is taken – either proactively or adaptively (reactively). It is a concept that belongs to the management side of the firm. It is management's way of guiding the future development of the firm. It is an attempt to specify the future potential of the firm in the market in relation to actual and potential customers. It is also the establishment of a general goal for the development of the firm such that this goal can be communicated to all employees, so they can follow the same path in their activities to bring about change.

The process of formulating a strategy takes as its point of departure market possibilities and the actual position of the firm in the market. The market relationship is the most important characteristic of the strategy (cf. Nyström 1990). The future market situation of the firm is fundamental to its future existence and the main criterion for how it should develop in the future.

Two other aspects are included in the basis of strategies. One is competitors. Strategy is also competition-related action where the movement of competitors plays a role. The firm takes the strengths and weaknesses of competitors into consideration when drawing up a strategy, and a later unexpected move by a competitor can make the firm adjust its strategy or, in extreme cases, change it completely. This is the perspective that Porter (1980, 1985) emphasizes in discussing strategy and it is also the basis of the popular SWOT model.

The consideration of competitors is natural and unavoidable when the future market is being analysed. However, this is only part of the market situation, which also includes other actors, primarily customers and their demands, but also, for example, political regulation authorities, suppliers and research institutions which could bring out new results. The basis of strategy is different in different firms. Some firms may focus primarily on competitors, but many focus on a broader range of external actors.

The service firms that I have studied – particularly financial service firms – generally focus mostly on competitors. They do not move (for example, by developing innovations) before their competitors move (Sundbo 1998a). According to service management and marketing theory, the customer is the most important actor. Service firms get most of their ideas for innovations from their interaction with customers. The firms that I have studied might have developed a more aggressive, innovation-oriented strategy if they had focused on the situations and needs of the customers rather on their the competitors.

Another aspect to be considered is internal resources. The implementation of a certain strategy requires that the firm has the right resources – employees, capital, organizational structure, technology and so on. The strategy must include a decision on this point: what resources are needed for the chosen strategy? Does the firm already have these resources? If not, how can it get them?

Internal resources are important; but if the firm does not possess a required resource, it can usually be obtained. I will come back to the relationship between the external situation – the market relationship – and internal resources.

2.3 Strategy as Interpretation

The premise of the strategic innovation theory is that firms have a top manager or a group of top managers (in the following called 'top management' whether consisting of one or more people) whose task is to form a business policy that is valid for a certain period; and further that these managers will consistently attempt to formulate such a policy.

In my empirical studies of service firms, they nearly all had a strategy that was an interpretation of the possibilities of the firm in the market in the future. The interpretations generally focused first on the movements of competitors, then came the possible needs of customers, the interests of shareholders and, finally, internal resources, including the competencies of the employees. In most of the firms the interpretation was done by the top management, but often involved some selected employees and middle managers. The top managers followed the strategy in their policy of developing the firm, but how consistently it was applied varied.

The view of strategy here is that it is an interpretative steering instrument for management (cf. Chaffee 1985). The strategy is developed as an interpretation of market development. The strategy concept in the strategic innovation theory is a combination of a market-oriented competition approach (cf. Porter 1980, 1985) and an internal-process approach (cf. Mintzberg 1994). Mostly the strategy is developed in a process where at least several top managers and often a number of middle managers and employees are involved. Mintzberg and Waters (1982) launched a number of models to show how this strategizing process can be conducted.

Strategizing is not considered here to be a fully rational process; it is a quasi-rational process. This means that management attempts to get as true a picture as possible of future market, future competitors and the future internal resources, but that it is not possible to arrive at objective truth. The interpretation process cannot help becoming hermeneutic (cf. Schutz 1967). Since no objective truth can be found about the future (that is, the premise is different from that of the strategic planning approach), the strategy is a series of signs or indicators of several possible futures interpreted through the perspective of the management. The top management, or the managing director, however, has to decide which interpretation to choose, and thus top management is responsible for the strategy.

As a starting point, we may assume that management interprets future possibilities as neutrally, and as much in the interest of the firm, as possible. Managers attempt to be rational, but this is not possible. That is also why strategies are changed from time to time, because the future turns out to be too different from what the originators of the strategy thought.

The formulation of strategy is, however, also a political process. Different actors in the firm – managers, shareholders, employees and others – can have different interests and these influence the strategy. This can lead to a complex strategizing process. There is the possibility that management may use its strategic interpretation as a power tool. Then the personal interests of management may be put above the interests of the firm. The strategy is at the same time an objective goal analysis and a potential power system. This entails that innovation, too, is potentially an object of power struggles.

2.4 Strategy as the Guiding Star for the Development of the Firm

The strategy process results in the adoption of a certain strategy, which becomes the management's tool for steering the future development of the firm. The strategy shows the employees and managers where the firm now stands and the way it wants to go in the future. It is the manager's checklist for development; he can use it to check whether the many changes are guiding the firm in the direction set up in the strategic goals. If the top management follows the decision criteria of the strategy, this shows the employees and middle managers what the top management wants and that it is following the strategy, and it thus becomes a visible, motivating force in the firm.

The strategy is thus a guiding star, and should remain so for a period. However, it may be wise or necessary to change the strategy, for example if market conditions change, if a necessary transformation of internal resources or organizational structure turns out to be impossible, or if innovations and changes open up unknown possibilities for another and better path for the firm. Internal political struggle may also continue in the firm, and the intrapreneurs (cf. Pinchot

1985) or innovation project teams may even attempt to launch innovations that run counter to the strategy. Strategy can therefore be a transient phenomenon and must not be defined here as a constant policy instrument that nothing can challenge. In some firms strategizing is a continuous process of struggle and change, but these firms will be a minority and will have serious difficulties in surviving.

The strategy may be formalized to a greater or lesser extent in written or theoretical form, but as a development policy it exists in most firms. The important thing is that management attempts to maintain a certain strategy or development policy and creates attitudes, makes decisions and intervenes in relation to it – not that the strategy is formalized. In many of the service firms that I have studied, the strategy was not formalized or written down. Nevertheless they had a strategy which guided the innovation process.

The interpretative model of strategy that I have launched here is expressed in the figure 5.1. The model is neither a purely rational one where the manager decides everything from a rational point of view, nor a purely processual one where all employees participate and no fixed goals exist. It is something in between.

Figure 5.1   Organizational characteristics of strategic models

Model	Determined by internal organizational behaviour	Dominant Interest	Form of Coordination	Conditions of Power
Rational model	One fixed goal Rational obtaining of goals	Technical, systematic	Centralist	Clear management dominance
Interpretative model	One fixed goal for some time, then a change of goals. Obtaining of goals through a general interpretation which needs operational implementation	Analytical, creative	Centralist, but interacting with the other members of the organization	Clear management dominance, which is challengeable and must be constantly legitimized
Processual model	No fixed goal; achievement of goals through social interaction within the organization	Professional, political	Decentral	Unclear conditions of power

Source: Sundbo (1998a).

2.5 Intended and Realized Strategy

Changes are thus made in the strategy from time to time. This raises the question of whether the realized strategy is different from the intended one, as Mintzberg and Waters (1982) and Nyström (1990) claim. The implication of this would be that strategy cannot be considered as a true management tool as stated here, and perhaps that strategy in reality does not exist.

There are various answers to this question. Mintzberg and Waters are right in the sense that if we take one official written strategy that is said to be valid for a period, we will often find that after some time the realized strategy differs from the intended one. This is caused by the adjustments that are made by new market situations, unsuccessful transformations of internal resources and innovations. However, management is not necessarily totally unaware of these transformations. I would argue that it rarely is. If it were, the top management would soon disappear, either removed by the board or because the company has gone bankrupt. In some of the service firms included in my empirical studies, groups or departments made their own policies which they attempted to realize. In most cases top management became aware of this and either suppressed it or changed the strategy so that the policy in question was included. In a couple of cases top management did not become aware of it and the situation ended with a struggle between the old top management and the rebellious group over the strategy that should be chosen.

These changes to the original strategy are thus part of the conscious adjustment that takes place from time to time, as argued above. Management will attempt to register adjustments and include them in the actual strategy. Thus what is important in the strategic innovation theory is the *actual* strategy, which is the one that the firm has at a given moment. It corresponds to the original strategy, which Mintzberg and Waters (1982) call the intended strategy, plus the successive adjustments that the management is aware of and has included in its policy.

Nyström (1990) also uses the dichotomy of intended and realized strategy and associates it directly with intrapreneurial activities within the firm. In his model it is the intrapreneurs who change the intended strategy and create another strategy that becomes the realized one. This view will be included in the strategic innovation theory, which will strongly emphasize changes in intended strategy through the intrapreneurial process. However, in contrast to Nyström's model, I presume here that management is an active partner in the innovation process and that the managers attempt to follow changes in the intended strategy continuously and act in relation to intrapreneurial activities.

In conclusion, the realized strategy often, but not always, becomes different from the originally formulated (intended) strategy. However, changes will normally be picked up and guided by top management, which will include it in an adjustment of the original strategy. Thus an actual strategy, of which the management is aware, will always exist.

3 ACTION, INTERACTION, ROLES AND DECISIONS

Strategizing is only the starting point and forms a general framework for the innovation activities in firms. The innovation process itself takes the form of actions and interactions in the firm. Innovation is an organizational process. The strategic innovation theory will thus be action- and interaction-based. This gives the theory a sociological basis which accords with the interpretation of evolution given earlier.

Why should we choose a sociological basis with action and interaction as core concepts when we are trying to understand innovation? There are several arguments for this. The innovation process has turned out to be a complex one that cannot be explaine, for example, by linear technological–economic models (cf. Kline 1985; Kline and Rosenberg 1986) or classic entrepreneur theory (cf. analyses in Kanter 1983; Pinchot 1985; Sexton and Kasarda 1992). Empirical analyses have shown that the complexity of the innovation process is due not only to technical and scientific problems, but also to the fact that innovation is carried out by people in social groups, that is, within the organizational structure of the firm and in smaller units such as project teams. These analyses have dealt with services (Sundbo 1997, 1998a; Gadrey et al. 1993; Hauknes 1998.) as well as manufacturing (Nyström 1979, 1990; Cooper 1988; Heap 1989). They demonstrate that the sociological character of the organization in which innovations are developed is crucial. Thus several theoretical analyses have emphasized the organizational structure of innovation in the firm as the explanatory factor for innovation (Burgelman and Sayles 1986; Mintzberg 1989; Burns and Stalker 1961; Hage 1980). This organizational structure includes intrapreneurs (Pinchot 1985; Sundbo 1992a; 1996).

It is also characteristic of the professional performance of the manager that he acts, but he also interacts. A hierarchy exists, but innovation cannot be managed by means of bureaucratic, hierarchical actions or technological–scientific logic alone. The manager therefore needs to interact with other people and other roles in the organization. This is a sociological process which has no deterministically predictable outcome.

All these factors indicate that the sociological character of the innovating organization is more important than knowledge, technological trajectories or individualistic factors such as the classic entrepreneur – which is not to say that these factors are unimportant.

The interaction may use various channels. It may be face to face, it may be person to person via information and communication technology and it may be through media (such as a company magazine). The most efficient and most frequently used channel is face-to-face interaction, because in that situation an understanding can be developed: knowledge can be understood better and each party will find it easier to learn about the thoughts and needs of the other party.

This is the most convincing form of interaction. Next comes information and communication technology. This is more efficient in the procurement of information, but when it comes to real knowledge – deeper understanding – it is only an auxiliary instrument, and face-to-face interaction is more efficient. Media communication is one-way and is the least efficient channel.

In this theory the manager has been designated as the innovation determinant. This means that he is also a sociological determinant. The manager is a person, but he acts as a professional, which means that he plays a role. He brings with him a preceding socialization, including his formal education. His professional socialization and competencies as well as his personal characteristics and socialization form the basis of his actions. This differs from the view of the classic entrepreneur as innovation determinant in that the manager's professional ballast is more important than is the case with the classic entrepreneur's. We have thus noted two things that are crucial to the strategic innovation theory: first, that role is a core concept in the theory, and will be used to analyse the system for organizing and managing innovation; and second, that we have defined the roles of the manager, the entrepreneur and the intrapreneur. The definition of these roles has been much discussed in innovation literature ever since Schumpeter's time (Schumpeter 1934, Drucker 1985, Pinchot 1985).

The strategic innovation theory has a fourth aspect: decision-making. Decisions must be made when a strategy is formulated and later if it is changed. Decisions are also made at different stages of the innovation process. Decision-making is tied to the manager, particularly to top managers, and is a power factor. Even though managers interact with other people in the decision process, they have to make the final decision. The manager thus gets power over the firm and other people in the organization, but he also assumes responsibility.

PART II

The Elements

6.   Market Orientation

The strategic innovation theory is a broad theory which encompasses many factors, internal and external. The core of the theory as discussed in this book is the internal innovation processes and the organization of innovation, but the main assumption is that innovation is primarily determined by the market (cf. Sundbo 1998b). Innovations are produced by internal processes, but the processes are triggered off by market possibilities and changes.

Firms have become highly market-oriented and customer-focused. This is particularly true of service firms, but increasingly of manufacturing firms too, as demonstrated for example by Normann (1991) and Gummesson (1999). The fact that firms – even manufacturers – are becoming increasingly market-oriented in their innovation activities (at the expense of an R&D orientation) is reflected, for example, in Kotler (1983), Nyström 1990, Tidd, Bessant and Pavitt (1997) and Porter (1990).

The assumption is, then, that this type of innovation theory is pull-oriented, that is, that the market potential is the crucial determinant. Most firms innovate when they can see new market potential or when there is competitive pressure in their market situation. Their innovation behaviour then becomes strategic. Courses of action other than innovation might be relevant in different situations (for example, price-competitive behaviour, rationalization of production and so on – cf. Porter's 1980 generic strategies). Innovation is one resource among others in the firm's attempt to survive and grow, and innovation could be replaced by other resources. However, innovation is one of the most important resources, and probably the most important. Innovation can make the firm take a giant leap in market competition.

A central question here is how the market determines the innovation behaviour of the firm. Can we set up a model for the way different market situations lead to certain kinds of innovation behaviour, and should I spend most of the book analysing markets? The answer is no. The fundamental assumption in this book is that we cannot deterministically predict innovation behaviour from the market situation. Markets cannot generally be predicted. If they could we would not have all the business literature that exists or the management problems that firms have. The relationship between the market and innovation behaviour depends on the concrete, current situation. Furthermore, the managers of the firm have to interpret the market situation and give their version of the firm's possibilities, and thus will create further different, unpredictable situations.

As mentioned above, I intend to combine the inside-out approach of the resource-based theory with the outside-in approach of the Porter theory. The approach here could be more precisely characterized as an out–in-management approach, which means that the market situation as well as internal resources determine innovation behaviour, but only through the management's interpretation of them. This interpretation is an action-oriented social construction (cf. Berger and Luckmann 1966) created by management. And the management formulates a strategy on that basis.

In this chapter I will offer a general introduction to this approach, which will be extended into a model describing the innovation process and its organization. In the following chapters I will first deal with external aspects and internal organizational ones.

Before I go on to market determination, I will briefly summarize why we have come to a stage where such a broad model is necessary to explain innovation.

1 THE BACKGROUND FOR THE STRATEGIC INNOVATION THEORY

Many developments have influenced innovation activities, and researchers have noted that an increasing number of factors are involved in the innovation activities of firms. Entrepreneurship and science-based technology development are no longer the only determinants of innovation. Looking for one determinant that can explain innovation might lead us to one core explanatory factor; but no such factor suffices to explain the total innovation process in firms.

Some of the most important developments that have led to innovation becoming a multi-factorial process are as follows.

- *Market saturation.* Many markets have become saturated because people and firms have had most of their needs fulfilled (cf. Sundbo 1998b). This makes it more difficult to introduce innovations in the market, and firms are forced to focus on many factors to develop more advanced innovations that have a chance of acceptance in the market.

- *Customer orientation.* Increased customer orientation, particularly as introduced by service management theory (Grönroos 1990, Normann 1991), has put the focus on market factors. The customer has become a central actor, as for example have social movements such as environmentalism.

- *Increased importance of service, and merging of service and manufacturing.* Not only the increased emphasis placed by service firms on innovation, but also the increasing importance of services to manufacturing firms, has widened the field of innovation factors. Many manufacturing firms add services to their goods (for example, financing, information, repairs, advice to the customers and so on).

- *Flexibility and modularization.* Production today has to be more flexible and modularized (cf. Sundbo 1994). This further means that process and organization innovations are becoming increasingly necessary.

- *Changes in society.* New political and ethical waves in society affect the consumers' preferences. New political and institutional trajectories (for example, EU regulations, deregulation, environmental movements) suggest ideas for innovations and make them necessary. This makes social institutions and public actors innovation determinants.

- *Knowledge is more important.* Innovations are becoming more knowledge-based, even in services. In manufacturing the knowledge base is broadening – it is no longer limited to technological and scientific knowledge. External actors such as suppliers (including consultants and technology suppliers) and public research and knowledge institutions are becoming important factors.

- *Technology is more important.* This is evident in manufacturing, but even there information and communication technology has become increasingly important over the last decade. In services, technology, in particular information and communication technology, has become more important as an innovation determinant.

- *Networks.* Competitors have always been an important innovation factor, because firms have imitated their competitors' innovations. Recently cooperation in networks has become more widespread. This is an advantage in many innovation processes and a necessity in some. The networks often involve competitors, but also public institutions, suppliers and customers. These actors have become important innovation factors.

2 MARKET-DETERMINED INNOVATIONS

New possibilities in the market can be seen by the firm and can make it innovate. The ideas for innovation often come from the market. Customers in particular are a source of inspiration, because products can only be sold if they fulfil the needs of customers. The inspiration for innovations is not only the ideas that customers express directly, but also general movements in society that may affect customers, for example 'the political consumer', environmental movements and so on.

Customers are also one of the most important partners in the development process when the innovation idea has to be developed into a practical, usable forms. They may be involved in the innovation process formally or informally. They may be involved as partners throughout the process or only in some parts of the process (for example, by testing prototypes of a new product or delivery system).

Market pull and the customer as an innovation determinant is an old element in innovation theory – even in the technology–economic tradition – and has been emphasized by several authors (for example, Kamien and Swartz 1982; von Hippel 1988). Empirical investigations in manufacturing as well as services have demonstrated that customers are some of the most important inspirers and partners in innovation processes (Sundbo 1998b). I have also found this in my case studies of service firms (Sundbo 1998a), although customers are not as important as one might expect from service management theory, which points to customers as the major determining factor in services. In particular, I found that many service firms did not involve customers efficiently in the development process.

Other external market factors are also important to the innovation process. The firm reacts to governmental regulation or deregulation and is inspired by general developments and events in society, for example through newspapers and TV. The most important market factor besides customers is competitors. The firm relates its innovation process to the behaviour of its competitors. This may include imitating competitors' innovations or behaviour, or the introduction of innovations to improve the firm's competitive situation. In my investigation of innovation in service firms, competitors were mentioned as the most important external innovation factor by the firms.

Innovation has been dealt with in marketing theories (for example, Kotler 1983; Baker 1985), which use the innovation concept as a kind of strategic concept. A firm innovates when the market makes it necessary, that is, when the life cycle of the product (cf. Vernon 1966) is running out, or when some competitors take a step that will endanger the firm's market position. Such a step might be an innovation, a new strategy or a new price policy. However, marketing theories say that the firm will only innovate when it is necessary to maintain its market position. This point of view can be supported by the argument that innovation is a risky process and most innovation projects fail. It can further be argued that the firm is not a social group that is brought together just to be creative and to innovate; that it exists to produce certain goods or services that are needed and which turn a profit. The firm should not risk its capital unless this is necessary, and it only does so when the sales curve actually falls or such a drop in sales is predicted. According to these arguments innovation is a necessity, not a type of behaviour in which the firm really wants to engage.

Another possible argument is that some firms at least are social groups that want to innovate. This is based on the fact that entrepreneurship exists among individuals, even in periods when business is going well. This is demonstrably the case, for example, with some present-day information and communication technology and software firms. They have chosen an innovation-based, aggressive strategy. Such firms exist and they must be classified in their own category (as front-runners – cf. Chapter 3). They may be a minority. Their death rate is fairly high, too, but those that survive sometimes show enormous growth in turnover and profit. Most firms are in the other categories innovating only when it is necessary to do so for market reasons. Of course even such firms sometimes get an idea for an innovation that puts them in the front-runner category, at least for a time and in one area.

This implies two things. First, it stresses that innovation behaviour is strategic, as already stated. The strategic behaviour of firms is primarily directed towards the market and competitors. Second, the internal resources and capabilities of the firm are major factors in the strategy, which must be based either on existing resources and capabilities or ones that the firm can procure. I will come back to this. However, first I will discuss market orientation as a strategic issue.

3 MARKET DETERMINATION AND STRATEGY

The firm has various possibilities if it wants to do well and grow in any market situation, and thus has choices. This is exactly what strategy is about. In the strategic innovation theory I am attempting to develop, the issue of market determination and strategy is viewed as follows: the market and the wider environment is the guiding star for the innovation process. However, because of the uncertainty of the environment, the firm cannot deterministically derive a single suitable strategy from an analysis of the market. It is dealing with a future situation that no one can predict accurately. Thus management has to choose a particular strategy and try to follow it until it turns out to be inappropriate. This is an inside-out marketing approach (cf. Duus 1997).

3.1 Innovation in Cycles

Furthermore, firms change their strategy according to their market situation. This leads to the assumption that the innovation behaviour of firms is cyclical (cf. Sundbo 1998a). Firms innovate when the market competition situation tells them to do so, and the cycles produce the successive strategic phases that the firm faces. Innovation behaviour follows the product life cycle (cf. Vernon 1966) although the firm must start the innovation process some time before the product life cycle slows down. Thus even if a firm has chosen a specific generic strategy, its innovation behaviour varies with the innovation cycle.

A model of the cycles is presented in figure 6.1.

Figure 6.1   Phases in the strategic situation of the firm

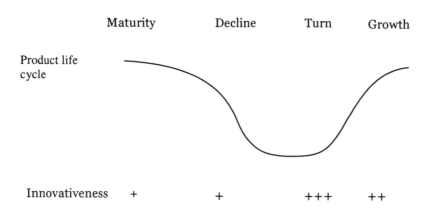

Innovativeness will increase in the 'turn' period to bring the firm into a growth stage. When this has been reached, innovation activities will decrease and the decrease will continue into the mature stage. However, this is a theoretical, ideal model. Firms will often not follow it strictly, because they are not fully rational entities but social systems where decisions depend on power relations, interactions and so on.

3.2 The Significance of Science

The market is thus the point of departure for strategic innovation. However, as already stated, not only market factors, but also internal resources and capabilities, are important. These will be dealt with in more detail in the coming chapters. The internal resource that has traditionally been emphasized in innovation theory is science. The above discussion could lead to the conclusion that science and knowledge are assigned less importance in the strategic innovation theory than in the mean technology–economic tradition. This is true of science, but not of knowledge. However, that does not mean that science is without importance. These views will be discussed in this section.

The strategic innovation theory breaks with the formerly dominant technology–economic paradigm in two ways (cf. Sundbo 1998b): (1) by not assuming that innovation processes are primarily pushed by R&D or technology; and (2) by not restricting itself to technological innovation.

R&D and R&D-pushed innovations, however, are not absent from the theory. Within each firm R&D-pushed innovation processes sometimes happen, and these will be a subcategory of the general innovation process. However, one of the assumptions of the theory is that even R&D-pushed innovations are steered by the strategy and thus by ideas about where the firm should be in the market in the future.

The weaker emphasis on R&D-pushed innovations is also due to the fact that social innovation plays a major role in the theory and this rarely has a linear development (cf. Kline 1985) based on activities in an R&D department.

It has been stated above that knowledge has a central place in innovation. This theoretical assumption has also been confirmed in my case studies in services (Sundbo 1998a), which showed that much innovation activity was based on practical and tacit knowledge (cf. Polanyi 1966), not on scientific laboratory experiments or investigations. This may be less relevant in manufacturing, but even there we hear of many innovation activities that are based on practical, tacit knowledge (cf. Nonaka and Takeuchi 1995).

Is this a theory of pragmatic innovation? Is science disappearing? Yes, to some degree. The idea that science – primarily understood as natural or technical science – is the only source for the creation of new products, markets, growth and profit must be rejected. Innovation has become a more complex sociological phenomenon, just as the fight against disease or pollution has – to cite some analogies.

This means that knowledge must be many-faceted: it must include knowledge of technology, but also of customers, societies, values, norms and so on. Practical knowledge is also important.

The picture of the typical innovation process is of a group of people who believe that there should be an innovation, but who do not really know what it should be. They have taken their point of departure in a problem that somebody else has, and they attempt to solve it by innovating (so that the firm can earn money). They do not just start up a laboratory experiment – at least they do not only do this. They look for all kinds of information and knowledge in many fields, including scientific and practical knowledge, that they can combine to get a more precise idea of the innovation they need and how it can be realized. Even in manufacturing most of the relevant knowledge is probably social.

Thus scientific knowledge is mixed with practical knowledge, and technical knowledge with social knowledge.

7.   External Driving Forces

After presenting the general view in Chapter 6, in this chapter I want to go a step further towards the diversified reality. I will present a model of the driving forces behind the innovation process. In this chapter I will only present the external driving forces; the internal ones will be presented in Chapter 9.

This is a general model of the environment. The driving forces do not determine innovation – as already stated, the interpretation is not highly contingency-based. The driving forces put pressure on the firm and thus have some determining effect on the innovation process, but they also open up the potential for the firm to create its own innovative path. This can either follow the direction of the driving forces or try to go against it.

What is actually done will depend on the strategy, which is the general action parameter. The strategy is a modifying factor.

1 EXTERNAL FACTORS: A MODEL OF THE DRIVING FORCES

External factors are more independent than internal ones. They are outside the control of the firm's management and have their own active life. That is why they are called driving forces. The innovation process is driven by external forces. These forces are social elements – people who act and interact, or active knowledge tied to people who act and interact. Thus they have their own active life independently of whether innovation takes place or not. Whether or not they are used actively as innovative assets depends on whether the firm wants to use them actively in an innovation process. However, external driving forces may bankrupt the firm, so it is well advised to take them into consideration.

Activation normally comes from top management, but can also come from particular employees (bottom-up innovation) acting on their own initiative. The success of activation is again dependent on the ability of the firm to activate the right forces at the right time.

The external driving forces can be summarized in a model of the innovation process. This is at the same time a model of the factors that can make management change its strategy. The model has been developed through work with innovation in services (Sundbo and Gallouj 2000). It includes many factors, but these were all found in empirical studies to be input factors to innovation in services. They are all relevant to manufacturing, too (perhaps with the exception of the service profession trajectory). The model is described in Figure 7.1.

Figure 7.1   Driving forces behind service innovation

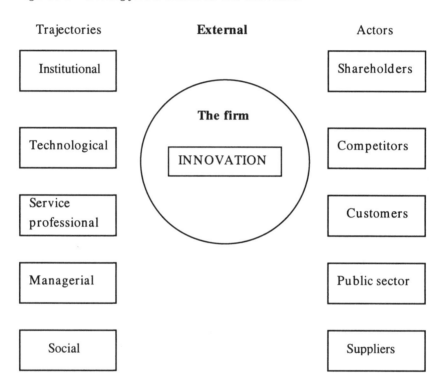

Source: Sundbo and Gallouj (2000).

The external forces can be divided into trajectories and actors.

Trajectories are ideas and logics that are diffused through the social system (a nation, an international network, professional networks and so on) (cf. Dosi 1982). They are the knowledge currents that exist in society and which the firm can utilize. This knowledge is often diffused through many actors who can be difficult to identify. Information and communication technology is currently a general means of procuring the knowledge, and increases the potential for seeking knowledge tremendously. However, the important factors are neither the information technology nor the actors but the ideas and logic behind the ideas.

We can identify five types of trajectory.

One is technology trajectories in the traditional economic sense (cf. Dosi 1982), that is the new logics for using technology which generally influence products and production processes. Examples are the information and communication technology the wave and more specifically the internet, or the freezer and microwave oven which together have created a new distribution system within catering.

Another important factor in services is service profession trajectories, by which we mean the methods, general knowledge and behavioural rules (for example, ethics) that exist in the various service professions (for example law, nursing, catering (how to cook)). This can also be relevant to manufacturing firms, since they too provide services.

A third type of trajectory is general management ideas or ideas for new organizational forms such as motivational systems, Business Process Reengineering, service management and so on.

The institutional trajectory concerns the general evolution of regulations and political institutions (for example, the European construct, European research programmes).

The social trajectory concerns the evolution of general social rules and conventions (for example, ecological and environmental consciousness).

These different trajectories are not independent of one another; in many situations they can be intertwined.

Actors are persons, firms or organizations whose behaviour is important to the firms' ability to sell products and services and thus to their innovation activities. The actors define market possibilities and are sometime involved in the development of innovations. They may also be obstacles to innovation.

Shareholders formally own the firm, and as such are important. Their influence is limited, and the shares are sold on a market, so they are in the position of being external actors. Their reaction to the firm's strategy and innovations, for example, is crucial to the potential for raising new capital for innovative investments from the market.

Customers are of course actors of major importance. They may be sources of information, but they can also contribute more actively to the innovation process. In certain situations the interface between the service provider and the client can be considered as being a laboratory in which innovation is co-produced. The customers' acceptance or rejection of innovations is crucial.

Competitors are also important to innovation activities. Service firms may imitate competitors' innovations, and it has often been a condition for starting an innovation activity that the competitors must move first. Competitors may also be collaborators in the innovation process.

Suppliers are important sources of innovation too. They may be knowledge suppliers such as consultants, or technology suppliers.

The public sector is the least important actor, but nevertheless an actor of some importance. The public sector demands services and goods, and delivers research and education necessary to innovation activities, but the public sector is rarely a direct actor in innovation processes.

Who are the most important actors? Different theories point to different actors. Porter (1980) emphasizes competitors. Network-based innovation theories (Håkansson 1987) emphasize suppliers and competitors (with the latter functioning both as competitors and collaborators). Service management and marketing theory (Eiglier and Langeard 1988) and some innovation theories (von Hippel 1988; Lundvall 1988) emphasize customers. In different situations, different actors may be most important. They may be important in two different ways – as strategic 'enemies' or as 'friends'. Competitors are always 'enemies' – even though as collaborators they also function as 'friends'; and political actors may be 'enemies' as well as 'friends'. Employees (or potential employees) may be 'enemies' (if they refuse to accept the innovation) as well as collaborators. All the actors may be 'friends' in some situations and 'enemies' in others. The relations between the 'friends' is expressed in the theories and models of strategic alliances, networks and so on (see, for example, Håkansson 1987).

The discussion above has focused on the firm's 'outgoing' activities. Strategy normally concerns sales possibilities, even in the theories. However, firms also have an interest in 'incoming' activities. They need knowledge from outside to develop innovations and create the best strategy. Knowledge is becoming increasingly important. Knowledge-procuring is rarely included in strategy theories (with a few exceptions, for example, Horwitch 1985).

Thus the strategic arena is complicated. The old, simple SWOT model is not adequate, although many firms still use it. It only emphasizes competitors; but many other factors are important in the market and other parts of the environment, as argued here.

2 THE INTERPLAY BETWEEN THE FIRM AND EXTERNAL ACTORS AND TRAJECTORIES

The enterprise interacts with external actors in the innovation process. This may involve formal cooperation where agreements have been set up, or simply interaction without formal agreements. In the latter case it will normally be certain employees or managers who interact with the external actors. The variations in the types of relationship can be illustrated, for example, by the relationship with the customers. An enterprise may draw up a formal agreement with a customer (a firm) stating that both parties will participate in the development of a new product; the agreement may specify the distribution of costs and of the profit that the innovation generates. It may also be an informal agreement where the customer is consulted about his needs and asked to assess a possible innovation; this can be done at different stages of the innovation process. Customers can also be used in a test of the prototype of a new product. The interaction with customers can also be hidden from the customer. An employee with customer contacts may have an idea for an innovation because he can see a problem or a need that this specific customer has, and which other potential customers have. This does not even need to be mentioned to the customer.

All the external actors specified in the model are involved in innovation processes. The firm interacts with these actors in different ways. Not all actors are involved in all innovation processes, and in some processes no external actors are involved.

The trajectories are all paths of knowledge transmission from the outside and are therefore all important. The relationship between a firm and the trajectories can also take several forms; it may be through the firm as an organization – when the management formally states that a trajectory will be used; or it may be an informal relationship organized by individual employees. Members of the professions, for example, have wide relationships with their colleagues in other firms and institutions, they read professional journals and so on. Individual employees can also note developments in a social trajectory by reading a newspaper or watching television. The interaction pattern between the internal organization and the external actors and trajectories is thus complex, with many different forms of relationship.

However, the decision about whether to develop an innovative idea is taken within the internal organization. It may be taken by the top management, and this will always be the case at some stage if the innovation process is taken all the way, but it may also be taken within the broader organization. If employees who gain new knowledge through an external trajectory do not think that it should be used for innovation, it will not be so used. Employees who want to act as intrapreneurs (cf. Pinchot 1985) can also look for information and knowledge through the external trajectories.

The external trajectories and actors cannot themselves explain the innovation patterns in the firms (as sometimes stated in the technology–economic tradition (see, for example, Dosi 1982)). All influences from the external system are filtered through the internal organization.

8. The Decision to Innovate: Strategy as a Modifying Factor

The driving forces do not produce innovations. They produce the conditions for innovations and put pressure on the firm to innovate; but the firm itself must decide to innovate before innovations can be created. This part of the innovation process will be discussed in this chapter. Strategy can explain this part of the process.

Strategy has two aspects. One is that it is market-oriented – the possibilities in the market guide the firm's development. The other is that it is decisive. The market situation itself does not automatically lead to a certain kind of innovation behaviour. Management must make the decision whether to innovate or not and when to do it – which is not very easy. In this respect strategy is a social act that can modify and sometimes even create a new direction for the driving forces, and thus external market forces, as was emphasized in Chapter 7. The strategy is a conscious action system that has the purpose of modifying the influence of external driving forces and guiding the action of the internal ones.

In the decision-making situation, management must look externally to see the nature of the market and of the external driving forces, and it must look internally to see the resources and capabilities that the firm possesses. These two inputs to e decision-making will be analysed here; the external one in this chapter and the internal one in the coming chapters.

1 POWER AND PROFIT AS THE FUNDAMENTAL MOTIVE FOR THE DECISION TO INNOVATE

The most fundamental motive for innovation is the desire for power and social position. Schumpeter (1934) described how the original innovator, the entrepreneur, was driven by the wish to obtain power, status and to demonstrate to others that he or she can solve problems, establish a firm and make it grow. Entrepreneurship is about power; first gaining power. Since we are in a market system characterized by competition, this means gaining power over others.

Even though winning power and status is the motive for the individual, it is transformed into a struggle for income and profit, since the individual operates in a business where power and status is correlated with income. The way to get income and profit is by solving a problem for society, or at least persuading citizens (or customers on the market) that their problem can be solved by this innovation (for example, that they will have a need fulfilled, or will get their commodities and services more cheaply).

The modern enterprise is rarely the same as the classic entrepreneur whom Schumpeter analysed. The latter played out his role as the dynamic factor in the economy a long time ago, as Schumpeter himself concluded some decades after his first analysis (Schumpeter 1943). Nevertheless the modern firm is driven by the same motives. These are primarily profit and the desire to increase turnover.

Even the established enterprise is often driven by power motives: for example the wish to be well-known, to realize one's own ideas and to demonstrate that the firm can be creative, solve problems and grow – the same motives as drove the classic entrepreneur. However, it seems odd to talk about the motives of an enterprise. An enterprise is not an acting person, even if it is described as such in economic theory. In the framework of the strategic innovation theory, an enterprise is just a framework – it cannot act. Those who act are the managers and employees. They act as individuals and as collectivities. This will be further analysed throughout the book.

2 THE STRATEGY AS AN ACTION PARAMETER

Economic theories of the firm posit various driving forces behind economic development. Generally they single out one of these as the core force, the elementary particle to which all explanations can be traced. Wilamson (1975) has transaction costs, Nelson and Winter (1982) have routines, the resource-based theory has core resources (or competencies) and the knowledge-based theory says it is the knowledge base. In this theory the 'elementary particle' is strategy.

Strategy is an action parameter. It is not a decision on a single innovation, because that is made in specific situations. Strategy is the general framework for decisions about innovations and change.

The innovation process can be explained in its most elementary form by the triangle in Figure 8.1, which expresses two aspects of strategic management, an external one (which has been treated in this and previous chapters) and an internal one (which will be dealt with in the following chapters).

Figure 8.1   Two aspects of strategic management

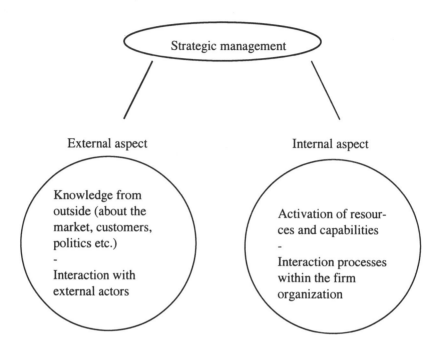

A question that may be raised is whether I am talking about the total strategy or only the part of it concerned with innovation. I am talking about the latter, since the strategy can include aspects that have nothing to do with innovation. However, the innovation part of it will generally be in accordance with the overall strategy. If it is not, there will be serious discrepancies in management policy, and management will have to adjust either one or the other. Thus the innovation part of the strategy may be assumed to be in accordance with the general strategy.

2.1 External Aspects of Strategy

The strategy expresses the market position that the management wants the firm to have in the future.

The management – either one manager or a group of managers – interprets the environment (as stated earlier). It does so on the basis of knowledge of its environment: customers' needs, preferences and problems; competitors' behaviour; possible political trends and so on. This knowledge is used by the managers to create a picture of the firm and its possibilities in the market in the future. This picture remains stable for a time. The strategy is the development guide for the firm. If it is changed too often, this confuses the managers and employees, and it is necessary to engage them in the development process.

The management forms the strategy on the basis of its knowledge of the external factors plus some creativity. The management can set up new goals. Strategy is a selection and decision-making process. There are always several possibilities, and managers must choose among these. These choices involve questions such as 'Should the firm emphasize product or process innovations (or some of the other types, or a combination)? 'And should it emphasize technological or social innovations?'

The management's interpretation, and thus the strategy, can be changed if the environment changes. The strategy can be changed by: (1) Actors (movements in the environment, by customers or competitors in particular); and (2) trajectories (new knowledge, inventions or technology development).

If such important factors appear, the strategic path can be changed. Whether and when it will be changed is up to the management. The characteristic of a good manager is that he can find the right moment to change the strategy.

2.2 Forms of strategy

The results of strategic considerations – how the firm relates to the environment – can also vary. The strategy can take different forms.

The firm can behave in relation to the market and the environment in two fundamentally different ways: offensive or defensive. The offensive strategy is used when the firm decides to take a step forward in growth and development. It intends to initiate hard competitive behaviour by increasing its own market share and reducing its competitors', or it intends to create a new market by innovating. The first situation might also involve innovation (which will then only be incremental). The defensive strategy is used when the firm is in a good market position: it sells well, but the competition is increasing. In that situation the firm will attempt to maintain its market position, at least for a while, without taking any risks. An offensive strategy is more risky than a defensive one because it may arouse the competitors and other actors in the environment, and they may reply with an even more aggressive strategy. If the offensive strategy involves innovations, that is also risky. Thus it is by no means always the case that the firm should choose an offensive strategy.

Generally, the offensive strategy is chosen by more innovative and flexible firms, while the defensive one is chosen by more stable, low-tech firms (cf. Nyström 1990). Or, as Burns and Stalker (1961) stated, the same firm may choose different strategies in different situations. This relates these strategic choices to different phases in the product life cycle (Vernon 1966) – cf. Chapter 6.

There are different offensive as well as defensive strategies as shown in Figure 8.2.

Figure 8.2   Different possible strategies

Offensive	Defensive
Product renewal	**'A little bit better' (minor improvements)**
Radical or relatively radical product innovations. Perhaps also the introduction of new quality standards.	Small improvements of products, processes, organization etc. or minor quality improvements
Professionalization	**Price leadership**
More knowledge-based and professional production. May involve recruitment of new professionals.	Reducing costs and profit to sell more.
Opening new markets	**Merger**
Finding markets that have never existed before, or adopting radically new market behaviour.	Merger and acquisition to create larger, more efficient units.
Market segmentation	
Definition of a new segment that can be aggressively worked on.	Withdrawal to a smaller segment of the former market with less competition.
Image creation	
A new image that signals aggressive selling behaviour.	Repairing 'scratches in the image'.
Political action	
Getting the political system to introduce standards and other regulations to one's own advantage.	Removing regulation barriers to further growth.

Other forms may exist or arise, since this is not a fixed situation and managers of the firms are creative and may invent new forms.

The offensive strategies emphasize innovation in products or behaviour, the defensive ones productivity and efficiency.

2.3 It Is All about the Future

Strategy is a long-term activity and is thus about the future. This makes it even more difficult, because the crucial thing is not the current environmental situation but a future one. It is a matter of what customers will want in the future as much as what they want now. The firm may influence customers' needs for the future.

The strategic moves of competitors will also be made in the future. This means that the managers of firms have to relate not only to the current situation, but even more to a future one that cannot be predicted accurately. The managers must choose the picture of the future environment in which they believe most, without being sure that it will be realized.

That is why managers are so interested in future studies and other attempts to look forward. They also have to take a broad perspective. It is not sufficient to look at historical consumption patterns, as market research has mostly done. General trends in society concerning norms, ideologies, behavioural patterns (general macro-sociological factors) and so forth are probably more important for the medium and long term.

3 THE ROLE OF ECONOMY

What is the role of economy in this strategic innovation process? The process has been discussed above as a creative, decision-oriented sociological process, but economy – costs, income and profit – is still the foundation of the firm.

It could be argued that economy is secondary to the creative sociological process. It could also be argued that economy is the foundation, but that it plays a less important role in specific decisions. The innovation process is by nature a qualitative process. It is driven by the possibilities of having ideas, solving problems and, for individuals, promoting oneself and getting power (as Schumpeter said in his first book, Schumpeter 1934). These are sociological and psychological motives. Innovation is a dare-and-risk process where the economic benefit cannot be assured, and certainly not calculated, so direct economic goals are not good incentives for innovation.

However, the firm is in general driven by economic motives – the desire either to increase turnover or profit, or at least to maintain a surplus. Economy is the ultimate driver of sociologically and psychologically driven innovation processes.

The ultimate goal is economic and is a controlling factor; economic considerations are used to decide whether to go on with an innovative idea or to stop. At different stages of the innovation process management must decide whether the prospects for income justify the development costs.

The economic benefit of an innovation project is doubtful and comes after the process has been completed – sometimes a long time after. However, some probabilities for the general outcome of different type of innovative behaviour can be stated.

9.   The Scope for Innovation

Having discussed market orientation as a point of departure, I will now go on to consider internal innovation factors. This discussion will be based on a model at the level of the firm, which defines the central elements of the theory and also defines a structure which will be used in the development of the theory. We are still at the level of a general model where management is considered as a rational entity at the top of the firm. The management's scope for innovation is thus an abstract model, more in the style of the economics tradition. The real social life of the management, with more nuances, will be discussed later, in the next chapter.

In this chapter I will present and discuss the elements of an abstract model of the innovation capacity of the firm. These are the principal internal factors related to innovation management and constitute the scope of the firm's innovation behaviour. They are the basis for the management's decision as whether or not to innovate.

1   A MODEL OF THE MANAGEMENT'S SCOPE FOR INNOVATION

This model includes elements from the discussion of the resource-based theory of the firm (for example, Foss 1997; Teece, Pisano and Shuen 1997). The model is composed of three elements. The idea is that the firm has a preparedness which is composed of two elements. One is a stock of resources that can be useful in innovation processes. These are physical resources (such as machinery, a workforce etc.), knowledge, and the abilities and competencies of employees and managers. The firm's external relations, too, are resources in this stock. The other element is the ability to organize an innovation process when necessary (dynamic capability). This is the ability to bring about creativity, interaction and entrepreneurship, the last of these in the sense that employees dare to take risks and struggle for their ideas. This could also be called a competence. However, the competence concept is not very precise as it has been used in economic theory. It is not quite clear whether it means only a resource and the knowledge one possesses, or whether the concept also includes the ability to use these resources and act. Nor is it clear whether competencies are individual or organizational or

83

both. Here I make a distinction between the passive asset, the stock or the resources, and the activation potential, the dynamic capability.

The third element is the ability to activate these resources and capabilities or to introduce new ones at the right time. This is a task for management. It is a strategic ability which the management controls. The activation of resources and capabilities may be supposed to be decided within the framework of the strategy.

A model can be set up as shown in Figure 9.1.

Figure 9.1   Managements's scope for innovation

Stock   **Resources:**
               Physical
               Economic
               Knowledge
               Individuals' competencies
               etc.
                                                    Innovation   Management
                                                    The ability to procure
                                                    the stock and activate
                                                    capabilities
                                                    - at the right time
Capabilities   **The ability to organize**   (strategic ability)
               the innovation process:
               Creativity
               Interaction
               Entrepreneurship
               Formal organizing

In the following two sections, the stock and capability concepts will be discussed and specified in detail.

2 THE STOCK

The resources or assets that constitute the innovative stock of the firm exist either as formalized resources or embedded in the employees. The resources can be of different types, and specific firms have specific resources that are of strategic importance to them. Some of the firm's resources are placed in the environment outside the firm, and are interactively related to it. The firm's image and position in the market could be one such resource. It exists in the market outside the firm, but the position and image are only maintained as long as the firm behaves in the right way.

It is thus difficult to generalize about which resources are important. It is also difficult for firms to know which resources will be the important ones in the future and even to know exactly which resources the firm has. Many resources are hidden because they are embedded in the employees. No doubt knowledge is a crucial resource, but even this can be of different types. Competencies in the sense of managers' and employees' experience, for example of running innovation projects, and their ability to act in the different innovation roles, are also important. Besides these, more traditional resources such as capital and existing technology are important.

If one were to venture to make a general statement, it would be that three assets are the main innovation resources:

* Knowledge (professional and technological knowledge, knowledge of the market and customers, society etc.)
* Competencies (the ability to act in the different innovation roles; for managers the ability to create and guide an innovation process)
* Capital

However, knowledge and competencies are very general concepts and the specific knowledge and competencies that firms possess vary greatly. These assets include an efficient training and education system, either internal or external. Even capital is not a fixed asset. If the firm does not have enough capital, it can go to the capital market and get it. In that situation other resources are crucial to whether the firm can raise capital, for example its knowledge base, management competencies, innovation tradition and so on.

Besides these a number of other resources may be important. Some of the most important are:

* Technology
* Buildings and other physical facilities
* Sales system (that is a sales organization that functions well and feeds its experience back to the organization)
* Position and image on the market
* Customer relations

- Relations to other external actors, including suppliers, competitors and political actors

3 CAPABILITIES

The innovation capabilities of the firm are its abilities to mobilize the innovation stock when necessary. Innovation activities are cyclical. In periods when innovation activities need to be intensified, such capabilities are crucial to the efficiency of the innovation process.

Four general capabilities form the foundation for innovation capabilities:

- The ability to define problems (which means the customers' or competitors problems);
- Creativity;
- The ability to procure knowledge; and
- The ability to organize the innovation process and encourage intrapreneurship.

These capabilities are part of a number of instruments that management can use to mobilize the right resources in situations where they are needed. The most important of these will be discussed in the following sections.

3.1 Strategy

The strategy defines the goals for the development of the firm and is thus an instrument for checking whether its development is on the right track. The strategy is also a means of activating entrepreneurial processes in the firm. It has a signal value for employees and managers.

The strategy functions as a guiding star for innovation. Normally, it does not include ideas for specific innovations. It may include proposals for certain types of innovations – for example, stating that the firm should emphasize process innovation in particular, or a certain type of product innovation – and it may state how innovative the firm should be. However, it mainly provides a framework for the innovation process. It says something about where the firm wants to go, and perhaps about how it wants to get there. It can provide guidelines for the entrepreneurs concerning how innovative they should be, and what types of innovation they should develop. It may also include inspirations for innovation and thus create an induced innovation process (cf. Binswanger et al. 1978).

The management's strategic interpretation may also be changed by internal factors – for example, if new resources or capabilities arise within the firm. It can be changed by new ideas from within the organizational structure of the firm; and by the management's own new ideas.

A very important capability is the ability to 'read' the market. This means to sense or analyse when the market is about to change, and to get an idea of the products, delivery systems and market behavior that could be successful in the near future. The top management may have this ability, or the marketing or sales departments may have it. The ability can be systematized in formalized methods or it can be intuitive.

3.2 Initiation

Systems for improving and activating creativity in the organization are important. There may be permanent idea-encouraging systems such as channels for employees to present ideas or permanent organizational development programmes (such programmes may involve permanent development and the learning of innovation processes). This was the case in many of the service firms I studied. There may also be ad hoc initiatives, where one or more managers can behave as leaders and inspirers and thus launch an innovation movement. This requires managers who have this ability.

3.3 Corporate Culture

Innovation-oriented corporate culture is often mentioned as a core capability for innovation processes (see, for example, Kanter 1983, Sjölander 1985). Intrapreneurship is promoted by an entrepreneur-oriented culture with norms suggesting that the generation of ideas and entrepreneurship are good, and it is impeded by an entrepreneur-hostile culture.

Innovative management action has the weakness that intrapreneurial activities must be cyclical. Sometimes intrapreneurship has a positive effect on the development of the firm; sometimes it does not. It is difficult to build it into the culture as a permanent value.

In my empirical studies of services (Sundbo 1998a), I concluded that there was no correlation between creative, initiative-promoting cultural elements and the degree of intrapreneurship. The factor that showed a correlation with actual intrapreneurship was the strategy – whether it signalled that intrapreneurship was desirable or not. Thus corporate culture is complex, and although it represents an innovative capability, it is a doubtful one, particularly as an instrument that management can control.

3.4 'Stop-and-go' Efficiency

A more efficient instrument is a 'stop-and-go' policy. Part of the management of innovation is the ability to know when to promote intrapreneurial activities: when these should be 'wild' and untrammelled and when they must be disciplined and put into fixed frameworks.

It is equally important to know when to stop innovation activities. This is a problem for the general innovation process – when to slow down – as well as for individual ideas – when to say stop.

This is a core element in top management's ability. It may be codified and systematized in experience-based decision models or it may be an intuitive ability that the management has.

3.5 Organizational Ability

In the stages of the innovation process that come after the idea stage, it is important that activities can be organized. The organization can take several forms – for example formal organizational units such as project teams or an efficient R&D department; or the task may be assigned to another department with experience of running innovation projects. It can also be a tradition within a more loosely structured organizational pattern, sometimes with no supervision.

Sometimes the organization has an ad hoc structure in the sense that some managers create a new type of organization either inside or outside the main organization. This requires that there are managers with the ability to start up new departments or venture companies (cf. Burgelman and Sayles 1986).

3.6 Activation and Procurement of Knowledge

The knowledge that exists within the organization – tacit as well as codified (cf. Nonaka and Takeuchi 1995) – is often passive. It must be activated for innovative purposes. Knowledge from outside must also be procured to develop innovations. In both cases it is important that management knows which type of knowledge exists within and outside the firm.

Another situation arises when people within the firm define some problems that must be solved to develop the innovation, but no one has the requesite knowledge. Then they must go outside the firm to seek the knowledge they lack. In this situation the knowledge of knowledge is of no use. What counts here is the ability to define problems and look into the unknown to find new knowledge. Sometimes the search pattern follows a trajectory, for example a professional or technological one. This produces a more stringent and disciplined kind of knowledge. Sometimes it follows non-traditional paths that can lead to creative and radical solutions.

The knowledge required is not only 'push knowledge', that is, ideas for solutions and new products and methods. 'Pull knowledge' of the market and customers is more important. Such knowledge may be found through scientific channels, for example marketing research, but very often it is found through other channels (such as TV programmes, newspapers, personal practical experience, consultants and so on).

3.7 Alliance Capability

The involvement of external actors is important. This capability can be based on long-lasting relationships, either formalized as agreements between firms or more informal, for example employees' relationships with employees of other firms, with institutions or with customers. These relations must be cultivated such that the external actors can be motivated to contribute to the innovation process.

The capability can also be based on ad hoc relations. There may be a situation where people in the firm want to get information from an external actor or to involve the actor in part of the development process. It may also be that the firm wants a certain service or attitude from the actor, for example a certain political decision from a political actor. Sometimes the firm wants to form an ad hoc alliance with external actors. In all these cases it is important that the firm, or some of its managers or employees, are able to inspire trust and motivation among potential partners.

4 INNOVATION MANAGEMENT

Top management has the task of selecting the resources (stock) and capabilities that should be used in a certain situation. It also has the task of maintaining these, either by creating them within the firm or by buying them from the market, or at least ensuring that they will be developed by the employees and managers. Thus the management holds the innovation system together.

The management, if its aim is efficient innovation management, will make sure it maintains the right resources and abilities and that it mobilizes them at the right time. Innovation resources and capabilities are expensive. It will therefore be most economical to maintain only those that are relevant at a certain time – although this is difficult in practice. This management decision will be discussed in the next chapter.

The formal leadership consists of the top managers who are appointed by the owners of the firm – for example by the board. There may be one or more managers, and a board of directors is usual in large corporations. This group of top managers constitutes the management. Even if there is a group of top managers, one person will be the uppermost top manager (for example, the managing director, but here I will call him the top manager). He may be the owner (if it is a one-owner firm). What I have been talking about so far is this top management.

The management (whether a group or one individual) can play a major or minor role in the innovation process; but it always plays some role. It is finally and formally responsible and normally it assumes that responsibility (although we can find cases where it does not).

The management may or may not have an innovative drive and may have greater or lesser interest in change, but currently it is a professional duty for every top manager to ensure that innovations are created in the firm. Management can do this by creating an innovation system. In some cases the top manager is himself an entrepreneur within the firm.

The management can be of different types: autocratic-hierarchical, more democratic, collective (as in partner-owned consultancy firms), entrepreneurial (one owner who decides) and so on. The type that is most innovation-procuring may depend on the situation, but in general an innovation-efficient management has the following characteristics: it is communicative and innovation-inducing; and it has a consistent strategy. There are exceptions inthe latter case, especially if a radical innovation is appearing. Then it becomes necessary to change the strategy.

10. The Organizational Structure: The Dual Organization

When the top management of the firm has decided to innovate, how is the innovation process organized? In Chapter 9, I discussed the top management's scope for innovation and the internal decision factors: resources and capabilities. This chapter begins the work of discussing and specifying the model for the internal organization of the innovation process, that is, how the process is managed when the situation indicates that innovation is required.

This does not mean, however, that innovation processes are viewed as wholly planned, top-down processes. It means that we are now going to discuss the life-cycle of innovation processes, which also includes loosely coupled bottom-up processes. However, as stated before, a firm is a specific social group characterized by goal-seeking behaviour, so even informal social processes such as bottom-up innovation must be guided. The management will attempt to control them – by starting innovation processes as well as guiding them and by stopping certain innovative initiatives from below.

In this chapter I will start by defining the internal driving forces in the innovation process and its main organizational structure. In the following chapters I will develop the theory to explain the process and the 'free life' of innovation and intrapreneurship activities.

1 THE INTERNAL DRIVING FORCES

The core of the strategic innovation theory is the model of the organization of innovation in firms – that is, of the internal driving forces. In Chapter 7 I introduced the general model for innovation in the firm, and the external driving forces. These can now be supplemented with the internal ones. At present we do not differentiated among types of firms with different ways of organizing the innovation process. That will come later.

No comprehensive, systematic assessment has been made of whether internal or external driving forces are most powerful in manufacturing, and the result would probably be different for different industries. One argument for an emphasis on the internal driving forces as the core forces is that, even if the external forces are the strongest, they must be interpreted and converted into action by managers and employees. There is an interplay between external and internal forces, and if internal processes do not work, there will be no innovations. One example of this is the observation that customers mean most as sources of ideas for innovations, followed by internal ideas (or the employees), in services as well as in manufacturing (cf. Sundbo 1998a; Hübner 1986, p. 107). However, my observations of service firms demonstrate that it is rare for customers to communicate their future needs directly to the firm; in most cases they do not know them or are unable to specify them clearly. What happens is an interactive process in which employees (including managers) play a major role. The ideas are developed by employees when they interact with customers and observe their daily life and problems. Thus the internal driving forces are the core of the innovation process.

1.1 Internal Actors

To supplement the model of the external driving forces, I can now add the internal ones in the model. This is done below in Figure 10.1, which has three elements.

Figure 10.1   Internal actors

Internal actors

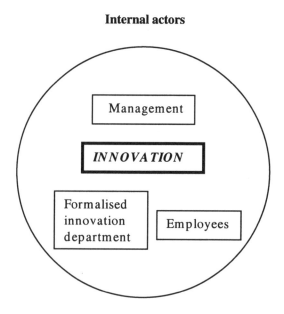

The internal actors are those who directly produce ideas for innovation, which is the precondition for the development of innovations. These are the employees, including the managers, who have ideas, and the formal innovation department. The management plays a role by inspiring, deciding on and restricting the innovation process. It also plays a role later on in the development process in organizing activities. The formal innovation department can also have this function.

The two most important actors are the employees and the management. This already follows from the logic of the strategic innovation theory as stated earlier. The formal innovation department plays a minor role. This element does not exist in all firms (if we take the total number of firms in any country, only a minority have such a department). There are firms where the formalized innovation department is the most important element (although these are still fewer), for example high-tech manufacturing firms. As stated before, the strategic innovation theory may not be valid for this type of firm.

1.2 Actors Become Structures

Within the framework of the strategic innovation theory, the single actor is not considered as an individual (as for example in classic entrepreneur theory). Individuals participate in a social interaction structure and thus operate in different kinds of groups. The interesting thing is not the individual actor, but the interaction structure. Employees do not act in isolation; their actions and ideas are generated in a social structure where they need to interact with other people. The formalized innovation department is not an individual, and in most cases not even a hierarchical structure which speaks 'with one voice'; it is a social system with different interests, conflicts and so on. Even the management is often, but not always, a group, and if there is one top manager who makes all the important decisions, he will – in most cases at least – interact with others before he makes his decisions. The interaction between management and employees is also important in the development of innovations.

Thus we must be interested in social structures, not in actors. The model above should be transformed into expressing the social structures that produce innovations. The organization is a structure, which has different sub-structures within it. Three of these are emphasized in this model. The internal elements of the model are social structures, which are networks of social positions that have relatively fixed tasks and ways of interacting.

In the model of the external driving forces, I defined actors and trajectories as the forces. The actors form the acting unit and the trajectories are flows of knowledge within a certain logic. The internal structures in the organization combine both in interactions. Each of these substructures is composed of actors interacting with one another and with actors outside the substructure (inside or outside the firm). The actors use knowledge from external trajectories, and even internal trajectories may develop. The point here is that the interaction pattern is as important as or more important than the logic of the knowledge – and this is where the strategic innovation theory differs from the economic attempts to grasp this (Dosi 1982, Freeman and Perez 1988). However, this only concerns the firm's internal trajectories. The external ones may still be understood from a knowledge logic as expressed in these economic models.

There are two core elements of the theory, the managerial structure and the loosely coupled interactive structure. These constitute a duality: each has its own life, but they also have a mutual relationship which is necessary in the innovation process. This duality is the most important aspect of the innovation process. I will call it the dual organization of innovation and will discuss it further in this chapter.

Now I can restate the model above in Figure 10.2.

Figure 10.2 Driving forces behind innovations

Internal structures

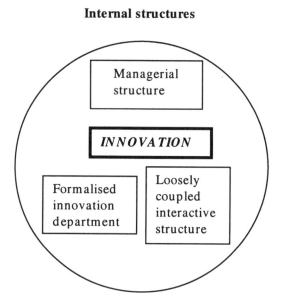

In the following sections each of the three elements shown in the figure will be defined in detail.

2 THE DUAL ORGANIZATION OF INNOVATION

The two principal elements of the innovation organization, the managerial structure and the loosely coupled interactive structure, have a life and a relationship which I have called a dual organization in my empirical analysis of innovation in services (Sundbo 1998a). This concept will be developed further here. The principle of dual organization means that two structures – in this case the managerial structure and the loosely coupled interactive structure – have their own lives, but are interdependent. Each needs the other to fulfil its task and each influences and intervenes in the other. The innovation process will be less efficient if the interaction between the two structures does not work, or if only one of them is involved.

The two structures are functionally, not physically, defined. Employees and managers cannot be divided into two separate categories in either the managerial or the loosely coupled interactive structure. The structures are functionally defined. All employees and managers have a role in the loosely coupled interactive structure, even top managers. The managerial structure is, however, more physically defined. It is a hierarchical structure in which each member has a clearly defined formal position that can be observed. Thus the organization of innovation involves a relationship between these two structures: The hierarchical managerial structure, shown in Figure 10.3, and a bottom-up system which is anarchic and with complex processes (shown in Figure 10.4); the system includes different roles.

Figure 10.3   The hierarchical managerial structure

Figure 10.4   The bottom-up system

● Roles

The dual principle of the model can be expressed as shown in Figure 10.5. It expresses the twofold view of innovation launched in Chapter 2 (Section 1): Schumpeter's (1934) creative – but also destructive – aspect of entrepreneurship, and Kirzner's (1973) coordinating and decision-making aspect. The loosely coupled interactive structure represents the Schumpeterian aspect and the managerial structure the Kirznerian aspect.

Figure 10.5   The dual principle

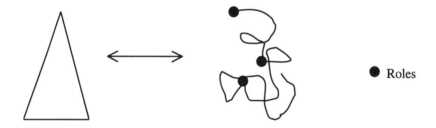

● Roles

3   THE LOOSELY COUPLED INTERACTIVE STRUCTURE

In this structure the network is not very fixed and stable. It is a loosely coupled network in which relations are often, but not always, temporary and loose. People may only have relations with one another in situations where concrete innovations are developed.

3.1 The Structure

Employees can act as intrapreneurs (cf. Kanter 1983; Pinchot 1985; Drucker 1985; Strategic Management Journal 1990). Individually they can have new ideas and struggle to get them accepted and developed into realized innovations. Many employees have entrepreneurial potential. In my investigation of service firms I found, for example, that in an insurance company there was hidden entrepreneurial potential that was not utilized among many employees and middle managers, particularly among the insurance agents who had contact with customers (Sundbo 1998a). Managers at all levels can also act as intrapreneurs. They too participate in the loosely coupled interactive structure.

The employee competencies that are important are:

- creativity;
- ability to structure an idea so it can become a product; and
- ability to fight to get the idea realized, and to communicate and convince other people in the organization that the idea is good.

The most important element in innovation and entrepreneurship is not having the idea or making the invention, but the struggle to get the idea or invention realized. There are many ideas and many creative people, but there is also great resistance to new ideas in organizations and other social systems.

However, intrapreneurs do not operate in isolation. They operate in a social structure that also has other positions and roles, and they depend on this.

The innovation process can be divided into successive phases (cf. the coming chapters). The loosely coupled interactive structure plays a major role in the initial phases. Innovations can be initiated by, and ideas can come from, the employees in various parts of the organization. The ideas come from below. This was generally the case in my observations in the service sector (Sundbo 1998a), and I assume that it is the same in manufacturing, except in high-tech areas characterized by extreme R&D push. This means that the innovation process depends on the creativity and initiative of employees (or managers).

The process of idea generation and acceptance is a social process where interactions play a role. Several employees or managers can develop a new idea in a group. The group does not need to be formalized; it may be people sitting together during their coffee break. Even if an individual develops an idea, he or she uses communication with other people to develop and shape the idea.

The acceptance of a new innovative idea is also a social process in which there are different positions, roles, alliances and conflicts, all of which are part of the loosely coupled interactive structure. Even though top management makes the final decision, there is a long process of convincing and acceptance in the organization as a whole before and afterwards.

The most important factor during the first acceptance phase, when the idea is diffused through the organization, is communication. The person with the idea and the intrapreneur must be able to explain the idea and convince people in the organization that it would be good for the firm. If they are not able to do this, or the employees are against accepting new ideas, the innovation process can fail right at the beginning, before the top management even hears about the idea.

The person with the idea sometimes gets an interested party to 'market' it. This person is called a 'sponsor' (Burgelman and Sayles 1986) or 'champion' (Pinchot 1985) and is often a manager or older employee who is not himself an ideas man.

This social system is the framework for the early 'social life' of an innovation. It is not a formalized system, but consists of scattered acts and interactions among employees and managers. It is a loosely coupled system where interaction patterns, alliances and conflicts are restricted to the development of the individual innovation. It is difficult to describe in one formalized model, except to say that various general roles can be found; but even these will not always appear. The roles and interaction patterns can shift within the lifetime of an innovation. Thus the only way to discuss the loosely coupled interaction system is to discuss different paths the processes may take. This will be done in Part III of the book.

In some cases the structure is not much in evidence. The originator of the idea or the one person who plays the role of an intrapreneur can go directly to top management and get his idea accepted. In that case, the loosely coupled interactive structure is either not activated at all or is activated by employees or managers as a defensive structure meant to resist the innovation or to modify it in accordance with their interests.

The loosely coupled interactive structure can thus also have a function in the later phases of the innovation process. However, it will normally be less important in these phases. Several roles and interaction patterns can be created in the later phases.

3.2 Roles

The foregoing discussion has shown that roles are an important factor in the model. It is therefore necessary to discuss which roles exist in the loosely coupled interactive innovation structure.

People play different roles. Some people play the same role all the time, and some change their role from time to time; many people play several roles at the same time. The organizational structure – the positions, the responsibilities and the formal-hierarchical relations – is important; but the main key to understanding the interactive innovation process is the different roles that individuals have.

Role is a classic sociological concept dating back to Mead (1934) and even further, and has been a core concept in micro-sociology and social psychology. The organization of innovation is considered to be a process in which positions, norms and habits are created. Members of the organization have different roles in that process. A role is a certain function which is executed in a certain way. Specific patterns of behaviour, and often norms and values, are related to specific roles. The roles may be created either by people themselves, in which case they are achieved, or by the leaders (in this case the managers), in which case they are ascribed (cf. Lundberg, Schrag and Larsen 1963).

The role concept is an analytical tool which is useful in structuring the behaviour of people in the rather anarchical process that is innovation. This tool makes it possible to impose some general structure on the process; not because the behaviour of each individual can be predicted, but because the existence of roles can be predicted.

Intrapreneurship is a role that is normally achieved either by employees 'naturally' creating their own intrapreneurship role or by the creation of a general innovative culture. The intrapreneur role can also be created by management through the strategy, the corporate culture and the development of the organization, a point to which I will return. Generally, intrapreneurs are still not 'appointed'; for this could be dangerous, because it is not easy to point out the individuals who will be the best intrapreneurs. This would involve a high risk of missing some innovations. The point is that intrapreneurship and innovations should come up from the bottom in an open and free process. There have been examples of attempts to ascribe an intrapreneur role to particular employees or managers. This may work in some situations, but often it does not.

Roles are different from the core factor in the classic entrepreneur theory (cf. Schumpeter 1934; Sexton and Schön 1986). The classic entrepreneur had a total, coherent set of norms, behavioural patterns and values that made him an entrepreneur. This was developed through the course of his life, and was often grounded in childhood (cf. McClelland 1961). It could be called a personality (cf. Sundbo 1998b) and the entrepreneur cannot shed his personality. Entrepreneurial personalities still exist, and should be taken into consideration. However, most effort in innovation processes in existing firms is made by people who are not entrepreneurial personalities. Nevertheless, they can play an entrepreneurial role. Roles can even be learned – cf. Drucker's (1985) theory of corporate entrepreneurship.

In my analysis of innovation in service firms I was able to identify three general roles:

1. The entrepreneur   - with a function in the innovation process
2. The analyst   - with a function in the strategy process

3. The producer   - with a function in the production process

These three general roles may be found in all firms.

Other roles related to the phases of the innovation process can be found, and have been discussed in the literature. Among these are:

*   The gatekeeper (looks for knowledge and other firms' innovations)
*   The idea-creator
*   The sponsor or champion (defined above)
*   The developer (who takes part in the development of the idea) with various sub-roles:
    *   The professional developer (for example, a researcher in a development
    *   department)
    *   The project manager
    *   The project member (who can have various roles in a project team, such
    *   as the person who proposes solutions to problems or the one who makes
    *   the other members cooperate)
*   The implementor (who implements the idea and 'sells' it to customers or employees)
*   The manager, who guides the whole process

4 THE MANAGERIAL STRUCTURE

4.1 Management as a Social System

Top management too is a social structure where several managers are involved in decisions and initiatives, although in some firms the top management, or even the top manager himself, makes all the decisions and there is no broad social system. Furthermore, even if the structure is a hierarchical one, managers at lower levels often follow personal interests, creating organizational policy and engaging in conflicts with each other or in relation to the top management.

This is the point where some irrationality is introduced into the management factor, which may hitherto have seemed relatively rational. However, this does not completely erode the rationality of the managerial structure. To a high degree it functions as a rational hierarchical system, as my case studies show. In some firms and in some periods innovation management may be an almost anarchic process, but this rarely lasts long, and if it does, it will very rarely lead to success. There are several stories of over-anarchic innovative firms that have gone bankrupt. This is not to say that innovation processes do not have strong anarchic elements, but to assume that there will always be an element of top-down control. How strong that element is can vary.

4.2 The Function of the Top Management and the Strategy

The strategy lays down the guidelines for the management, as already stated. It may function as an inspiration for innovations, but it also limits the types of innovations that are wanted, and can also be used to decide upon the concrete innovation ideas. Not that managements never accept ideas outside the strategy. They sometimes do; many quite radical innovations that can be very useful and profitable to the firm arise in this way. Nevertheless, the strategy is a general instrument for making innovation decisions.

The strategy can be more or less offensive in relation to innovativeness, as discussed in Chapter 8. It can also specify a certain customer segment, product or quality segment and so forth. It may include a vision and a mission and perhaps a scenario for the situation of the firm and the kind of firm it wants to be in the future. One important role of the strategy is perhaps its signal value for the employees, showing where the firm wants to go. This value is even greater if the strategy has been developed in a collective process in which many employees and managers have participated.

Nevertheless the strategies are rarely very detailed, so managers have wide scope for interpretation and independent decision-making. Then innovation management becomes an ongoing policy-making process where the managerial structure has to interpret the strategy when specific cases arise.

The top management can choose the principal paths for the innovation process. It can choose the R&D path, which means that innovation processes will be R&D-based and the development of the innovation will be handed over to the R&D department. That is the specialist approach. It can also choose the bottom-up or employee-orientation path, which means that the development of the innovation will be based on the active participation of many employees and managers from many departments and groups. This is common in services (Sundbo 1998a; Sundbo and Gallouj 1999). Finally, it can choose the top-down path, which means that management gets the ideas and organizes teams or other ad hoc organizational units to develop them.

The success of the firm depends on the top management's ability to make the right choices. However, the other internal driving forces, the loosely coupled interaction structure and the formal innovation or R&D department have their own lives, which means that pressure for innovations could come from them.

4.3   Innovation management at lower levels

Innovation management involves managers at lower levels. The top manager often consults other managers before he decides. Sometimes the task of creating an innovative social climate, collecting ideas and making the first decision is left to one or a group of middle managers, who are given the formal responsibility for the innovation processes. These may for example be personnel managers (if it is an organizational innovation) or the management of an R&D or other specialized innovation department.

Middle managers have a function in interpreting the strategy and overall goals. Ideas and initiatives need to be promoted in all parts of the organization. In this process, too, middle managers have a function.

Another task of the managerial structure is to restrict the innovations so that the firm will not waste resources on failed innovation projects. The innovation process should be balanced (Sundbo 1996).

The competencies that managers must possess are those that are generally required in a dynamic firm. These are different from the competencies that are needed in a firm with a steady production system and no product shift. Change and development in the firm requires a dynamic leadership style. If the manager does not signal dynamism, the employees do not perceive that dynamism and innovativeness are serious issues. The top managers do not need to be creative and innovative themselves, but they have to signal that these characteristics are wanted within the organization.

Some managing directors are top entrepreneurs – that is, they are entrepreneurs themselves within the firm (as found in Sundbo 1998a). This often makes the innovation process complicated because they attempt to dominate the process without being able to make all the innovations and develop them themselves. The innovations become images of their thoughts, and other ideas can have difficulty being accepted (even though they may be profitable for the firm).

Dynamic innovation processes cannot be planned, so the leadership should be flexible, with some intuitive elements.

5   THE RELATIONSHIP BETWEEN THE TWO STRUCTURES

The two structures have a mutual and interactive relationship, as stated above. Each needs the other. Top managers cannot have enough ideas themselves they need to involve the employees. On the other hand, if there were only the loosely coupled interactive structure, there would be no restrictions on the resources used on intrapreneurship and innovation activities. This would not contribute to the survival of the firm. Thus the functions of the loosely coupled interactive structure need the managerial structure.

Each also influences the other in the innovation processes. Ideas coming from below in the loosely coupled interactive structure may make managers think in new innovative ways, and this may even be transmitted through the managerial structure to top management. The top management must leave a certain scope for these activities in the loosely coupled interactive structure. It must ensure that a certain number of ideas are produced in the loosely coupled interactive structure and that a certain number of people want to play an intrapreneurial role from time to time. The employees and middle managers are empowered (Kanter 1983; Sundbo 1996), which means that they are allowed to present innovative ideas and even to fight to have them realized, that is act as intrapreneurs. Here – in contrast to Kanter's theory (1983) – empowerment is assumed to be restricted and controlled.

Innovation processes in the loosely coupled interactive structure can also be induced (cf. Binswanger et al. 1978), which means that idea creation and intrapreneurship are encouraged by the management. Inducement does not mean that the managerial structure directly produces innovative ideas in the loosely coupled interactive structure, because it is rarely able to do so. It means that activities in the managerial structure inspire the employees and give them a feeling that innovation is possible and required. Thus they dare to, and are inspired to, present innovative ideas. This process is a widespread and often unstructured one in which many employees are involved. It is not possible, nor would it be desirable or efficient, to control this process too narrowly. It is a creative, intrapreneurial process, which should be free and open.

On the other hand, the managerial structure creates initiatives and restrictions in the loosely coupled interactive structure.

Reciprocity also applies in the restriction process. The managerial structure restricts innovative ideas, as argued above. However, the loosely coupled interactive structure also restricts innovations. There can be cases where this structure – the employees in general – are against an innovation idea from the management, or where some people in the organization fight to realize an innovation that the managerial structure is against.

Generally one must assume that the two structures are in harmony, but sometimes they may be in conflict, as in these situations. The typical conflict is when the idea of an intrapreneur coming from below is rejected by top management, or the intrapreneur thinks that the top management will reject it. Then he may attempt to realize the idea anyway. One example from my case studies of such a situation was where a group of employees and middle managers used a big customer as an alliance partner in forcing top management to accept a new product idea.

Daft (1987) has demonstrated that a similar innovation pattern can be found in administrative organizations. He also operates with a managerial structure. However, there is a great difference between his second structure and the one discussed here. He operates with a professional structure – people from a certain profession – as the structure other than the managerial one, while I operate with a broad social structure in which many or all employees and managers take part. Daft's model is also more of a division-of-labour model where the managerial structure develops administrative innovations while the professional structure develops technical ones. Here I operate with the two structures as active in all kinds of innovation.

6 FORMALIZED INNOVATION DEPARTMENTS

Even though the third internal factor, formalized innovation departments, has been called the least important one, it can play a role in the innovation process. I will therefore discuss this role in this section.

6.1 The Department as a Social Structure

Some firms have a formal innovation department. It is formally a part of the managerial, hierarchical structure in the sense that top management can decide on the activities in the department. However, it is classified here as a structure in its own right because it has a special task and is therefore often outside the managerial structure. It often has great independence and has its own life because it is staffed by professional specialists who spend part of their professional lives with specialists in other firms and public institutions.

In manufacturing, the formalized innovation department is normally an R&D department; in rare cases service firms also have an R&D department. This can be a department that conducts research. However, very often it does not conduct strict research but is a development department that develops new ideas into implementable innovations. The innovation department can collect knowledge and buy technical elements from outside to develop the innovation. R&D departments are normally restricted to technological product innovations. They can deal with process innovations, particularly in relation to the development of a new product, but this is not always the case. Sometimes the necessary process technology is developed in the production department afterwards.

6.2 The Formalized Innovation Department Interacts with the Other Two Structures

This kind of department interacts with the other two structures. Even if it has its own life, it is forced to interact with the managerial structure in deciding which types of innovation to develop (to ensure that they remain within the framework of the strategy) and which steps to take in the innovation process (because each new step entails investments).

It also interacts with the loosely coupled interactive structure. At present most firms attempt to open up the closed professional culture of such departments and involve the rest of the firm in the R&D activities, particularly in the development aspects. The more the department is oriented towards practical development, the more it can be assumed to be intertwined with the firm's general activities; and the more research-oriented it is, the more isolated it can be assumed to be.

Other types of innovation apart from technological product innovations, are normally developed in departments other than the R&D one. This is the case with non-technological (social) innovations such as organizational and market innovations, and it is also often the case with technological process innovations.

R&D departments thus account only for a part of the innovations. In manufacturing, particularly in high-growth, high-tech industries, they can be an important element in the innovation process. There the important innovations are technological product innovations. However, in other manufacturing industries other types of innovation play a greater role, and R&D departments – if they exist – are not so important. Many innovative ideas do not come from the R&D department, and some innovations are even developed fully outside the R&D department, supposing that one exists.

In some service firms I have observed a particular type of innovation department actually called an 'Innovation Department' (Sundbo 1998a). These departments are different from R&D departments. They are not staffed by experts who are doing 'laboratory work' in experiments that could lead to innovations. An 'Innovation Department' is a kind of communication department. It has the task of promoting ideas among employees and managers, collecting these ideas and presenting them to top management for decisions. If the management decides to go further with the idea, the Innovation Department is rarely involved in this development process. The work in the Innovation Department requires communicative skills – the ability to promote ideas among employees and persuade them to give their ideas to the department. Often the department is related to the strategic department or is the strategic department itself. It is often placed just under the top manager and reports to him. This also means that the task of the Innovation Department is often dominated by its role as a strategic 'watchdog'. This role may dominate over its role as intrapreneur procurer, thus slowing down the innovation process, as was the case in several service firms. Functions like this can exist in manufacturing too.

The Innovation Department should consist of people who are experts in influencing processes in the loosely coupled interaction structure. It may also function as the intrapreneurial employees' spokesman to the top management, as the personnel of the Innovation Department can be assumed to identify more with employees than top managers do.

However, the Innovation Department also has the task of selecting innovative ideas, normally by using the strategy as the framework for decision-making. This function should be very carefully balanced with innovation-inducement functions so as not to hinder the appearance of innovative ideas. This balance is very difficult to maintain, and in my case studies I found that several of the innovation departments became more strategic controllers than idea-inducers, which is non-optimal.

7 CYCLICAL INDUCEMENT OF INTRAPRENEURSHIP

This has consequences for the cyclical innovation behaviour of the firm, which was introduced in Chapter 6. Since roles are the core factor in the loosely coupled interactive structure, the managerial structure (where top management has the final responsibility) is led to create and restrict specific roles which are different at different stages of the cycle. This cyclical role-inducement and restriction will be discussed at two levels. The first is the overall level of the degree of innovativeness – which means the allocation of resources to innovation activities; the second is the character of the intrapreneurial role.

7.1 Optimal Allocation of Resources

In Section 3.2 I defined three roles, each of which is associated with a particular type of activity. The distribution of the three types of activity – and the respective roles – can be assumed to vary with the strategic phase cycle.

In the following I will present a model of the actual allocation of resources distributed over the different types of activity (see Figure 10.6). The model is based on the empirical results in this and previous chapters and on subsequent theoretical analysis and further development. The inspiration has been attempts to formulate phase models for the industrial innovation process (van Duijn 1984).

Figure 10.6   Phases in the strategic situation of the firm and activities/roles

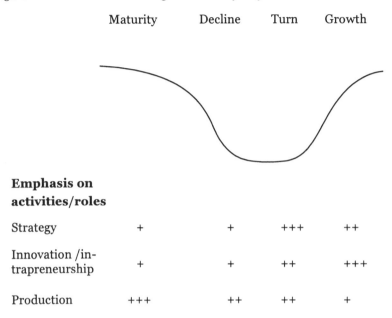

	Maturity	Decline	Turn	Growth
Emphasis on activities/roles				
Strategy	+	+	+++	++
Innovation /intrapreneurship	+	+	++	+++
Production	+++	++	++	+

The strategy is most important in the 'turn' phase and then decreases in importance. Top management is responsible for the strategy and makes the final interpretation, but it needs input from the organization. Thus it uses the managerial structure as well as the loosely coupled innovation structure to get that input. Several strategist roles are created in both structures.

Innovation or intrapreneurship becomes increasingly important in the turn phase; its importance peaks in the growth phase and then drops during the phases of maturity and decline. The role or activity of production is at its most important in the mature phase and then decrease in significance. This discussion is developed further in Sundbo (1992b).

The next question relates to the dual organizational structure, namely whether the managerial structure will be stronger than the loosely coupled interactive structure in specific situations. It can be assumed that this is the case. The managerial structure will be stronger in situations that include a phase shift and thus an increased emphasis on new activities and other roles. In such situations it will be rational for management to attempt to encourage the new form of role behaviour and to inhibit the old. In situations which do not involve a shift, it could prove an advantage to let the loosely coupled interactive structure play a more dominant role. This includes the collective processes in the interactive structure.

In a phase where innovation and intrapreneurship are required, the company might achieve the best innovation development if the free intrapreneurship of the loosely coupled interactive structure made its presence strongly felt.

7.2 Optimal Regulation of Intrapreneurship Roles

This analysis has a particular interest in intrapreneurship roles. When are they mainly activated? It might be assumed that the firm develops varying degrees of limitations on intrapreneurship activities, as described in the model in Figure 10.7.

Figure 10.7 Phases in the strategic situation of the firm and intrapreneurship roles

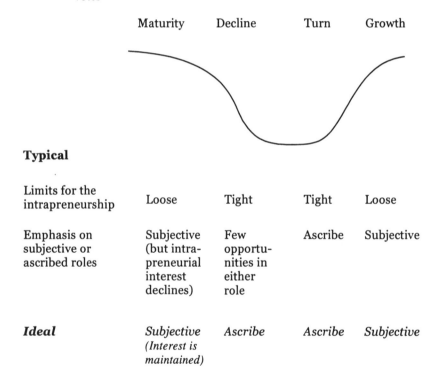

	Maturity	Decline	Turn	Growth
Typical				
Limits for the intrapreneurship	Loose	Tight	Tight	Loose
Emphasis on subjective or ascribed roles	Subjective (but intrapreneurial interest declines)	Few opportunities in either role	Ascribe	Subjective
Ideal	*Subjective (Interest is maintained)*	*Ascribe*	*Ascribe*	*Subjective*

The strategic phases are described as a cycle (cf. the product life cycle). Increased innovation activity in the loosely coupled interactive structure and entrepreneurial personalities are accepted as the company moves into the 'turn' phase. The phase still has tight limits, since the resource consumption of the company is vulnerable to over-expenditure on innovation processes. It is assumed that this describes the normal course of the cycle for most companies. Theory would claim that it would be a better course of development if companies prepared for an increased innovation effort during the growth phase by maintaining an innovation system during the mature phase and then strengthening this system in the decline phase by creating a number of ascribed intrapreneurial roles. Companies would then follow the course indicated by italics in the model. This discussion is elaborated in Sundbo (1992b).

7.3 Cycle Models as Rational Abstractions

These models remain rational abstractions. The model can be said to be rational, since it describes the allocation of resources (although at a general level). The model does not however rest on the assumption that resource allocation is a quantitative hierarchical process in which management can mathematically allocate financial resources in measured doses. The model expresses the qualitative conclusion that the consumption of time for each activity and the incentives for performing the different activities will undergo phase shifts.

In real life, companies will not be able to operate in such a rational manner. They will often have difficulty controlling the processes which should take place in both structures. Sometimes the loosely coupled interactive structure is superior to the managerial structure in picking up signals and initiating changes. At other times new roles cannot be developed within the interactive structure.

In the next part of the book I will develop in detail how we may suppose that firms operate in practice in the innovation process, and look more closely at the operation of roles, on the basis of my case studies in the service sector and other empirical results.

This does not preclude the possibility that such models have a certain value as guidelines in practical management as well as in scientific understanding. Since I intend to develop this theory close to real life and on an empirical basis, however, I will at present leave abstract theory aside.

PART III

The Innovation Process

11. General Model of the Innovation Process

In the previous chapters I have defined the elements of the innovation process. In this and the coming chapters I will be looking at the innovative life of firms. This will take us down to the micro level: the innovation situations where the innovation activity is carried out as a social process. This is a complex matter, because there are different patterns and forms of organization in different phases of the innovation process and in different types of firm. The model must therefore be divided up. The phases of the innovation process will be the criteria as these are what separate processes most. The differences between firms are not that great (according to my empirical results, Sundbo 1998a; and also according to the general results of manufacturing studies – cf. Freeman and Soete 1997; Tidd, Bessant and Pavitt 1997). The variations among firms will be dealt with in the discussion of individual phases. This part of the analysis will also include more empirical examples.

In this Chapter I will discuss the innovation process in general: that is, the social processes – norms, values, behaviour, interactions – that go on in the enterprise and which may result in innovations. I will state some fundamental principles for how the innovative social system functions.

The following analysis of the process will be structured in three parts, defined on the basis of different phases of the development of an innovation. Each of these parts will be discussed in turn in the next three chapters.

1 THE FUNDAMENTAL PRINCIPLES

The social innovation system functions on the basis of certain fundamental principles which have been stated in the foregoing chapters. These principles will be used here in order to formulate a general model for the innovation process.

The most fundamental principle is that innovation is an interactive process. Several individuals and parts of the organization participate in the innovation process, and they interact with one another and with external actors.

Another fundamental principle is the dual organization. There are two poles in the innovation system. One is a rational pole, which is the managerial structure. It attempts to make innovation processes goal-oriented and cost-minimizing. The goals are economic (increased turnover and profit), but may also be non-economic, such as procuring a good image for the firm or putting it in an advantageous strategic situation which may not produce any current economic benefit but may do so in the future.

The other pole is a non-rational one, the loosely coupled interactive structure. For employees and managers (in this structure) the effort is not economically grounded, nor does it have a clear purpose for the firm. It could have, but in most cases it does not. The effort is social. Employees want social prestige or power within the organization, or they are occupied with solving a problem. That is why they make an effort in the innovation process. They may seek personal rewards, but these are far from always being financial. In my case studies (Sundbo 1998a) the most desirable reward was independence (cf. also Pinchot 1985). The intrapreneurs wanted freedom in their work, meaning a situation where management would not intervene very much. This could be obtained by their being appointed managers, but often it was just a matter of being allowed to spend their time on their projects without supervision. Often the employees, and particularly the managers, considered innovation activities as part of their daily work – simply an unremarkable everyday activity. They made this effort because they thought it was fun or interesting, or they saw it as part of their normal work. The effort is rarely determined by rational considerations. If it is, it is often driven by personal, career-strategic considerations, not firm-strategic ones. This makes the process of involving employees difficult and complex. The management has to fulfil certain of the goals of the individuals' strategies to get them involved in the innovation process.

The polarization in the dual organization is not extreme. Even though the managerial structure tries to act rationally, this is not possible, as already mentioned. There are too many unknown factors for fully rational management behaviour, and this is even more true in innovation. The managerial structure therefore acts only in a quasi-rational way, as already stated. The loosely coupled interactive structure is, on the other hand, characterized to a certain extent by rational behaviour. Employees and managers sometimes follow the goal of creating the greatest possible growth for the firm, perhaps trying in this way to achieve personal goals. They may infringe the norms and values of the social system if this is necessary to realize their innovative ideas and this may create conflict and polarization in the organization.

That is also why a strategy is necessary for the firm. It keeps employees and managers on a certain path of development. The management can administer the strategy by rewarding the right innovative behaviour, but there is also an element of constraint in its behaviour. The top manager makes decisions about the employees' and managers' innovative ideas and behaviour.

These fundamental principles lie behind the concrete variants of the innovation process that will be dealt with in the following sections.

2   A GENERAL MODEL FOR THE INNOVATION PROCESS

In Sundbo (1998a) I have developed a general model of the course of an innovation process based on case studies. The model states how much the process is individual, that is, how much innovation is driven by individual intrapreneurship, and how much it is organized, that is, in a collective interactive process (whether managed by the managerial structure or as a 'free' interactive process in the loosely coupled interactive structure). The model is expressed graphically in Figure 11.1.

Figure 11.1   Model of the innovation process

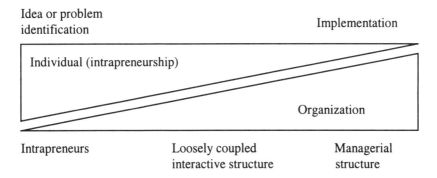

The model describes the innovation process from the first idea generation or problem identification through its development to the implementation phase which results in the innovation being realized (a product is sold on the market, an organizational development is completed and so on). The innovation process is mainly dominated by individual effort at the beginning, then it becomes increasingly organized, which means that the loosely coupled interactive structure takes over. Later the managerial structure takes over. The first step, the individual effort of the intrapreneur, often takes place in interaction with other people, but this model explains the relative importance of individual and organized effort in the different phases of the process. The first idea phase is not always individual; the innovation may be initiated by management and a formal organization established from the beginning. The later phases may be carried out by individual intrapreneurs, although that is rare. The theoretical statement is that the pattern described in the model is typical of firms that can be described in terms of the strategic innovation theory. Empirically this statement can be supported by my case studies in the service sector (Sundbo 1998a).

3 THE PHASES OF THE INNOVATION PROCESS

The path of the innovation from idea to implementation, and thus the innovation process, is expressed in the model. The process can be divided into a number of phases. In the following chapters I will divide it into three phases:

1. *Initialization.* In this phase the problem that is to be solved is identified and the first idea is developed. It also includes the first entrepreneurial struggle to get the idea accepted.
2. *Development.* The first idea is often vague. After it has been accepted, it must be developed into a type that can be implemented in practice.
3. *Implementation.* When the innovation has been fully developed, it must be implemented in practice (a new product must be produced, a process or organization innovation must be implemented etc.).This phase is often forgotten, but it is important because there can be much resistance here, and it is here that many innovations fail.

Throughout the process – perhaps apart from the very first initialization phase – the process is under the constant control of the formal managerial structure, which seeks to take the leading role. At least, top management attempts to do this. However, sometimes it fails, as will be discussed.

The model and the phases are abstractions that serve to structure the field. There has been some discussion, and severe criticism, of the linear model in the technology–economic innovation theory (Kline 1985), which sees innovation as a straight-line process starting with invention and ending with implementation. It is not intended to introduce a linear principle into the strategic innovation theory. In practice there will be a lot of back-loops, blind alleys and mixing of the phases. The innovation process is also different in different types of firms. The phases are only used as a mean of structuring the fundamental social processes in innovation. If we do not have any structuring principle, everything will be chaos and no theory can be generated. The variations will be discussed in the next few chapters.

12.   The Initialization Phase

This phase is important because having the original ideas and getting them accepted by the organization is difficult.

In this phase the innovation process can go three ways, that is, the first development of an idea and the struggle to have it accepted can happen in three different structures – those that we have defined as the internal elements of the innovation process: the loosely coupled interactive structure, the managerial structure and the formal innovation department. As stated earlier, the managerial structure will interact with the other two structures. The interaction between it and the loosely coupled interactive structure has been termed the dual innovation organization. This is still the most important aspect, since most innovation processes are assumed to develop in that kind of relationship. However, many innovations start in an innovation department. In such cases the managerial structure will also attempt to take control quickly, so the interaction between the innovation department and the managerial structure is relevant to this theory. Often, after the initialization stage, the innovation process will be taken over by a more complex structure, typically a project team in which the innovation department is one participant. This gives the interaction of the loosely coupled interactive structure, the managerial structure and the formal innovation department a role in the innovation process.

Thus the initiative and the first development of the idea can go three different ways:

1. It can comes from below (the loosely coupled interactive structure) – often with the management as inspirer
2. The management can initiate the process (among other ways by using the strategy)
3. It can take the formal R&D path (the initiative comes from an innovation or R&D department)

These will be discussed in turn in the following three sections.

1 INITIATIVE FROM BELOW

This is the most important approach in modern firms (at least outside high-tech manufacturing firms, but even there it may be the most important) and forms the core of the strategic innovation theory. It will therefore be given most emphasis. It is an approach that uses ordinary employees, but also managers at various levels. In the loosely coupled interactive structure, many small, unreproduced ad hoc changes happen because employees often face a situation where a problem appears. The problem must be solved, either by the individual employee or group of employees who have the problem, or by someone else in the organization. This situation starts off two processes: creativity in individuals and groups – the search for an idea that will solve the problem – and an interaction process to see if other people can contribute to its solution. When a solution has been found, this particular problem has been solved and no one thinks any more about it. An innovation initiative may also begin with an employee who simply has a new idea for a product, a process or another type of innovation. He or she may be inspired by reading newspapers or journals, by observing activities in everyday life or from some other source.

Although I have said that the ideas come from below, top management can play a role in the process. It can create a climate or culture that improves intrapreneurship and it can inspire it. It does not create the innovative ideas itself, but it does create a system that encourages the employees to have ideas. This has been called induced innovation (Binswanger et al. 1978) and is not considered here as a top-down innovation process, but as part of the interaction in the dual organization.

1.1 Ad Hoc Changes and Innovation

How and when will this unreproduced change be transformed into a reproduced change – into what has been defined as an innovation? This happens if someone later encounters the same problem and asks around the loosely coupled interactive structure; the first solution is then communicated and implemented once again. If this happens several times, it becomes a reproduced change and thus an innovation. It may also be the case that someone thinks that thew first solution should be communicated throughout the firm and implemented in similar situations. This will also make it a reproduced change. Finally, we have the situation where someone gets an idea for a new product, process or kind of market behaviour and tries to get it accepted in the organization. This is a process of reproduced change from the outset.

However, many small changes remain unreproduced. Taken together they do develop the firm, but in an uncontrolled and unknown way. One can assume that management will attempt to observe all these unreproduced changes to ensure that good solutions in one situation can be used in other, similar, situations. Often they do not. However, they often do. That is why firms establish learning systems in which they try to store the solutions, a point I will return to in Chapter 15. However, this is extremely difficult to systematize and organize, because the process of change is anarchic. The best the management can do is nurse the loosely coupled interactive structure in the hope that new ideas will be communicated in the organization and picked up by somebody who will reproduce the change. This is an ideal model and in many cases it does not work in practice. The management does not nurse the loosely coupled interactive structure; it either does not know how, or is unable to change a conservative interaction structure. The latter case may require a change in the corporate culture. These are the reasons why so many firms are bad innovators.

Why can we not simply rely on the routines discussed by Nelson and Winter (1982)? Can the management not steer the process by the introduction of innovation-oriented routines? This is one approach, but it is not sufficient, and routines cannot guide all changes. Many changes are answers to small, ad hoc, but unusual problems where routines do not help. The changes are outside the routines and are made at an informal level. The solutions also demand creativity; and free, informal interactions in the loosely coupled interactive structure and routines do not always help to improve this; they are in fact often an impediment.

1.2 Creation of Innovative Ideas

Innovations, as well as unreproduced small changes, are created by individuals who play an idea-creating role. In some cases these individuals act as full intrapreneurs by carrying the innovation the whole way through: They develop the idea and the new product (or whatever the innovation might be) to an implemented stage and they struggle for their idea. However, in most cases they only play a partial role as initiators and then the collective organization takes over (cf. the model in Chapter 11) – although they often become members of this collective organization. Even in the initial phase the interaction system is important in most cases. The idea-creator develops the idea in interaction with other individuals in the loosely coupled interactive structure. The idea is in many cases developed by a group within this structure.

It may be employees at the lowest hierarchical level who play the role of idea-creators and sometimes of intrapreneurs. However, my case studies in the service sector (Sundbo 1998a) showed that very often it is either middle or top managers who play these roles. This may vary from case to case. For the sake of convenience I will simply talk about employees in the following discussion, but this should be understood to mean employees and managers.

The new idea may be just an idea for a new product, process, organization, market form or use of raw material that an employee or group of employees (or managers) has. The sources of inspiration can be many – for example, newspapers, scientific articles, suppliers, interaction with professional colleagues or innovations by other firms.

Often, however, the idea will be a solution to a problem. The problem could be a production problem, a problem that a customer has, an organizational problem such as low productivity or organizational conflict, a sales problems and so on. Innovation is the answer to a problem. An innovation is developed if the employee or group goes through the following two steps.

1. *Definition of the problem.* This will nearly always be in interaction with other people. They may be other employees (or managers) or customers, who are empirically the greatest inspirers (Sundbo 1998a). Often the employee sees that the customer has a problem of which he is perhaps not aware. This becomes an inspiration for the employee to define the problem and look for a solution. The interaction may also be with other actors outside the firm (cf. the model of the external driving forces). It may also be with other people, for example friends and family members, who inspire the person to see that there is a problem in society that has not been solved. Problem definition requires certain competencies from employees (and managers). They must be (cf. also Majaro 1988): (1)Curious; (2) interactive; (3) sensitive; (4) observant; (5) reflecting; and (6) analytical.

2. *Solving the problem.* Solving the problem requires the development of the new idea. This in turn requires that employees (and managers) be: (1) imaginative; (2) knowledgeable - or able to obtain knowledge (external trajectories and information and communication technology will often be used); (3) communicative (able to obtain knowledge and perhaps allies); (4) systematic (in formulating solutions); (5) decisive (able to decide which solutions to continue with); and (6) goal-oriented and willing to struggle to achieve the goal.

The organizational conditions required for step 1 to arise and for the process to move from step 1 to step 2 are as follows:

- *Creativity and entrepreneurial spirit in the employees and managers.* Creativity requires a critical attitude and the courage to see problems, and an unconventional imagination in order to see solutions in a new way.
- *Problem and change-oriented organization and organizational culture.* The organizational culture may be: (1) bureaucratic ('stick to your job'); (2) political (all problem definitions are interpreted as a manifestation of interest);

(3) entrepreneurial (in the sense that the owner is an entrepreneur and does not accept other entrepreneurs); or (4) problem-oriented (it is permitted to be critical and creative in order to solve problems). The problem-oriented culture is the most innovative and is the one that mostly leads to an innovative, loosely coupled interactive structure. The entrepreneurial culture is innovative too, but not as much, because it is completely dependent on one individual entrepreneur. The bureaucratic culture may be innovative if it has an R&D department, but not as much as the problem-oriented culture.

- *Practical knowledge and experience.* If an employee has great practical experience, this will improve problem identification because he may associate the new problem with earlier problem identifications. The new situation may be similar to these.

- *A reward system.* Intrapreneurs, or people who play a partial role in the innovation process, only act in that role if they feel that they will get some reward for their effort. This has been demonstrated in a case study of a Danish bank (Sundbo 1999). The reward does not need to be money – it can be of different kinds, as mentioned earlier.

- *Quality-orientation.* This is not a condition for innovation, but it helps. If the organization in general is oriented towards quality problems, employees and managers are likely to be so too. This increases the problem orientation.

- *Change- and innovation-oriented strategy.* If the strategy is innovation- and change-oriented, it will inspire employees to see the problems and look for solutions.

The next issue is the solution of the problem, or – if the innovation is based on an idea that is not an answer to a problem – the further development of the idea. In this phase knowledge becomes crucial, as well as creativity. Theoretical and scientific or other trajectorial knowledge is of little use when one has to identify problems, but when a solution must be found and an idea developed into an innovation, it can be useful. However, it is not essential. An innovation can be developed on the basis of practical experience and intuition, but it can also be developed on the basis of theoretical and scientific knowledge. In this case (innovation from below), employees and managers define the problem and select the kind of knowledge they need to obtain. It is a situation of knowledge-pull, not knowledge-push.

Knowledge has been divided into tacit and codified knowledge (cf. Polanyi 1966). The former is the knowledge that individual employees have and which is not embodied in any formal media. The latter is knowledge that is systematized and embodied in formal media. Both are important in the innovation process, but in this form (innovation from below), tacit knowledge is particularly important. Even tacit knowledge only becomes really important in the problem solution stage. Problem definition is a creative process. Tacit knowledge may be of help there, but creativity can often run counter to tacit knowledge, which is a stock of earlier experience and thus may be a conservative factor.

The internal interaction process – both as a creative and a knowledge-procuring process – may use information and communication technology networks as media. This could increase the efficiency of the process, but whether it is a good instrument for convincing other people about an idea depends on the organizational culture. The more the data and information approach to communication and knowledge (which is the logic of this technology – cf. Davenport 1993) is accepted, the more this medium can be used. The more the personal-interaction knowledge approach is emphasized, the less it can be used.

The solution to the problem – or the further development of an idea – can be carried out in several ways.

1. *Entrepreneurial*. The idea-creator plays the full role of an intrapreneur and carries out the innovation all the way through alone, often with the loosely coupled interactive structure in opposition. Even the managerial structure may be in opposition. This is possible with small ad hoc (unreproduced) changes, but it is unusual with reproduced innovations.
2. *In the loosely coupled interaction structure or formalized team*.
    a. *Legitimation*. The idea-creator is allowed to carry the innovation through and is legitimized by the loosely coupled interaction system and perhaps even the managerial structure.
    b. *Informal interactional*. The idea-creator is allowed to carry the innovation through, but in an interaction system and under social control from the loosely coupled interactive structure, or perhaps from the managerial structure.
    c. *Formal interactional*. A project team with the idea-creator as a member is formally established by the managerial structure.
    d. *Colonization*. The collectivity – either the loosely coupled interactive structure or the managerial structure – takes over the idea and ousts the idea-creator. The innovation process is later formally organized.
    e. *Diffusion*. The collectivity takes over the idea quietly and develops it; no one can really tell afterwards who has done what; perhaps the idea-creator cannot even be identified (which was the case in some banks – cf. Sundbo 1998a).

1.3 The Role of the Managerial Structure and Strategy

In this approach to innovation development, the innovations come from below. Nevertheless, management plays a role in the process. It plays a crucial role in developing the organizational culture. Even if one does not assume that management can create a corporate culture (as Schein 1984 and other authors suppose), it can destroy the culture. The management creates, or must at least accept, the conditions for innovation processes that come from below (cf. above). New ideas and problem definitions may appear even if the management is not change and innovation-oriented, but the later stages – problem solution and the development of the innovation – will very rarely be realized if the management is against the idea.

The management can also to a greater or lesser degree create diverse incentives for the employees' intrapreneurship. This may vary from the creation of isolated tools such as sites in information technology networks where ideas can be discussed, to huge programmes of organizational development.

Thus management plays a role by signalling either an entrepreneurial and innovative orientation or the opposite. The strategy is a tool for such signalling and expresses what management expects from the employees. The more the employees have been involved in the strategy-formulating process, the more the strategy functions as a guide for action. The strategy is also a means of steering this balancing act: it may indicate the desired degree of innovativeness, for example, by being more or less offensive or defensive in terms of development and change.

Management plays a role not only in the initiation of changes, but also in the inhibition of change. The rationale for this follows the innovation cycle, as discussed in Chapter 10. However, it is not only in mature periods that intrapreneurial and innovative activities may have to be restricted. Even when an enterprise is in a market situation which mainly requires innovation, it cannot survive an unlimited degree of idea creation and intrapreneurial activity. This could use up so much of its resources that the enterprise would run the risk of going bankrupt (cf. the empirically based argument in Sundbo 1998a p. 283). The management needs to balance the intrapreneurial activities (cf. Sundbo 1996a). It comes in very early in most innovation processes and decides in the case of each new idea whether to go ahead with it or not. The process of innovation from below can be rather anarchistic in the early phases – although it is generally less anarchistic than it looks. The loosely coupled interactive structure is a social system that to some degree regulates people's behaviour. There exist certain norms, habits, accepted roles and so on that influence employees' behaviour. It is not a strong social system. The employee can for example seek support from the managerial structure to engage in intrapreneurial behaviour, or to try out an idea that is not accepted in the loosely coupled interactive structure. Nevertheless, this structure influences employees' intrapreneurial behaviour. Whatever the case, the management wants to have control over the innovation system. It does so by demanding to know about new ideas and to make decisions about their development at different stages of the innovation process. In most enterprises management has the power to do this (although individual intrapreneurs can still succeed in some situations in avoiding management control).

Management control of the innovation process from below can be expressed in a funnel model (cf. Sundbo 1996a, 1998a p. 197):

Figure 12.1   Model of management controle of the innovation process

Ideas and struggle to gain acceptance for ideas

| Idea not accepted | Idea accepted for decision | Idea accepted for decision | Idea not accepted |

Decision to innovate

Development of the innovation

Commercial marketing or internal implemention (if process or organisational innovation)

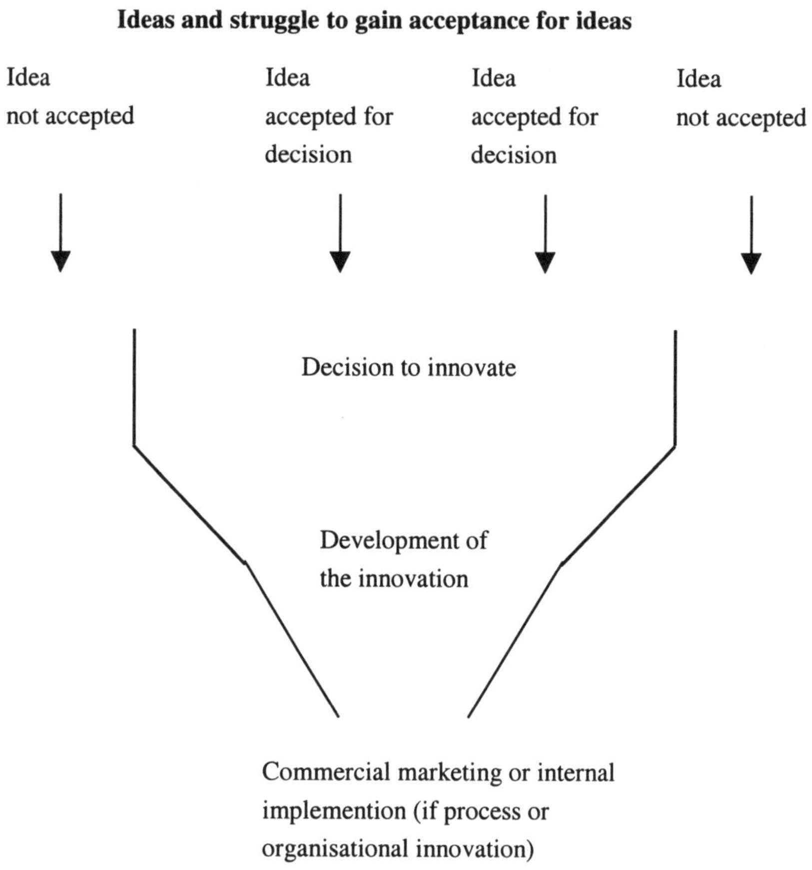

Different – often loose – ideas are presented from below. Some of these are selected by the managerial structure for continuation. Of the selected ideas, several are rejected at later phases. Thus very few result in realized innovations.

The strategy is used by the management as one guideline for making these decisions. It is not the only guideline, but it is an important one, and it is often used by the management if it is uncertain about an idea. It is particularly used by management to legitimize the rejection of ideas. This is an ongoing strategic-political process in which the development track of the firm is sometimes changed, either within the framework of the strategy or by breaking away from it. In making its decisions, management gives consideration to external actors because their future reaction to the intended innovation is crucial to its success.

1.4 Balancing Mechanisms[1]

In this section I will present some mechanisms that top management uses to guide the dual organization and the innovation process. They are called balancing mechanisms. The development of this model is based on my case studies (Sundbo 1998a). The mechanisms will be divided into two categories: inducement mechanisms and control mechanisms.

1.4.1 Inducement Mechanisms

Some inducement mechanisms are traditional core factors in innovation theory. Other influential factors were also found in the case studies. Even with respect to traditional factors, the case studies did not always come up with the same results as those generally referred to in the innovation literature.

Openness and networking

In the literature, the evolution of innovations and entrepreneurship is often described as depending on the organization's openness to the environment and its participation in external networks (Burns and Stalker 1961; Peters and Waterman 1982). This is obvious in service and low-tech firms – although in my case studies these types of firms were often very closed; this was because it is easy to imitate products and processes, particularly in services. It may also be an important innovation factor in high-tech industries where one scientist can speak to a professional colleague outside the firm.

---

[1] This section has been published as part of an article in *Technovation* (Sundbo 1996). It is published here by agreement with Elsevier Science Ltd.

Empowerment of customers

The involvement of customers has been stressed greatly in innovation research over the last decade (for example, von Hippel 1988; Lundvall 1988). Thanks to service marketing theory (Grönroos 1990; Eiglier and Langeard 1988) the focus on customers has increased. This may also be extended to innovation activities. Customers can provide central input into the innovation process because they can identify the problems that the innovations should solve – and perhaps the solution too. Empowerment is often extended to customers.

Generally speaking, the empowerment of customers is difficult (as my case studies showed). Customers sometimes suggest ideas, but often they are only involved in the testing of the prototype of a new product. This is because customers only have problems, very rarely solutions. Firms may learn something about their problems, but they cannot directly get new ideas for solutions from customers. Employees may observe and communicate with the customers, and develop their own ideas from there.

Empowerment of employees

General trust in the employees, communicated throughout the organization, and the delegation of responsibility for getting ideas and trying to act as intrapreneurs – in other words empowerment (cf. Kanter 1983) – is a general instrument for inducing intrapreneurship. The empowerment is expressed in the strategy and the corporate culture.

Strategy

Strategy is the core instrument in the inducement to innovate. It can inspire innovations. How it works depends on the kind of strategy that the firm has. If the firm has a very offensive market strategy, this particularly stimulates entrepreneurship activities related to the development of new products.

The empirical results of my case studies showed that strategy is not used for this purpose anything like as much as it could be. The control aspect of the strategy is assigned more importance. Here we have a kind of innovation potential that is often not utilized efficiently by management.

Corporate culture

The importance of an entrepreneur-oriented corporate culture is evident, and has been stressed by various authors (for example, Peters and Waterman 1982; Kanter 1983). This means that there are entrepreneurial values in the informal organization – what has here been termed the loosely coupled interaction system.

However, the Danish case studies found that an entrepreneur-oriented corporate culture as such was not the primary explanation of the innovation activities. Firms did not generally stimulate maximal entrepreneur-oriented cultural values, and when they did it became dangerous because of the loss of resources (including money). In the most successful innovation processes there was an entrepreneur-oriented corporate culture, but it was subordinate to the strategy, which formed the cultural values. The strategy became the framework for how much entrepreneurship there should be, and how it should be executed. Even though employees in some situations opposed the strategy, most intrapreneurs adapted the cultural values of free entrepreneurship to the strategy and other signals from the managerial structure. Even in consultancy firms, the entrepreneurship culture was becoming more disciplined and more subordinated to a strategy.

Rewards

Entrepreneurial profits or other types of rewards for intrapreneurs have been assumed to be essential to the procurement of entrepreneurs (see, for example, Burgelman and Sayles 1986). This assumption has been developed within the framework of economic market theory where individuals are driven by the chance of making a profit.

However, as already mentioned, intrapreneurs mostly seek other rewards, such as freedom in their jobs, promotion and so on – or innovation is simply considered an integral part of the job and therefore does not require any reward. This was also evident from my case studies.

Innovation department

An innovation department should stimulate and collect new ideas, encourage entrepreneurship and support entrepreneurs.

It can also develop new ideas and innovation projects itself, but can only go through the first stages of the innovation process. If a development stage is reached, the innovation process is passed on to another organizational unit, typically a project team.

Top entrepreneur

The existence of a top entrepreneur – as shown in my case studies – means that intrapreneurship, not only from the top manager, but from all employees, is generally encouraged. There is an extraordinary degree of innovation activity based on intrapreneurship in such firms. Most of it is done by the top manager, but some of it is done by employees and other managers. The extent to which employees are broadly empowered cannot be assumed in these cases to be among the highest or among the lowest.

Practical instruments for stimulating intrapreneurship

Various instruments for stimulating intrapreneurship were used in the firms I studied. Primarily, idea generation was stimulated. The instruments used for idea procurement were internal magazines, internal marketing, particularly through middle managers, and traditional suggestion boxes. The last of these in particular brought in many ideas. Not only the instruments as such were important, but also the general impression created by these instruments – that the management wanted entrepreneurial activity. They functioned as a sign of empowerment.

1.4.2 Control Mechanisms

Economic and time-consumption control

Economic control of innovation and empowerment activities is practised from a traditional economic point of view, but is very difficult. All the firms I studied attempted to have some economic control over their innovation activities. Economic control was in particular sometimes successful in the late stages of the innovation process, where the innovation has been developed into a completed business project – but not always. These stages were generally organized by means of project teams.

However, the problems were mostly found in the early stages of the intrapreneurship process. Innovation activities, in particular intrapreneurship activities, are by nature impossible to plan in economic terms. It is not possible to foresee exactly what resources will be needed or how far an innovation project will succeed. This is even the case in the late stages of development, although then it is a little easier to control economic factors. Intrapreneurship where many people are involved is particularly difficult to plan. If one is lucky, it is possible to count the resources spent in economic terms after an innovation project has been completed. However, even that is difficult, because employees engage in intrapreneurship activities together with their other activities. The intrapreneurship activities cannot be clearly identified, limited and accounted for in financial terms.

Thus economic control is of only limited value. Another possible way of controlling intrapreneurship activities is the use of time studies and time budgeting (cf. Sundbo 1992a). One method is to ask the employees and managers to estimate how much time they spend on entrepreneurship activities.

Strategy as a control mechanism

Thus a 'softer' or qualitative control mechanism is needed. As we have seen, the strategy can fulfil this function, as it defines the framework within which the innovations must be kept, and thus prevents the firm from using resources on unwanted innovations.

Decision-making stages in the innovation process

The strategy as a control mechanism is supplemented by successive decisions made by the management concerning whether to go on with an innovative idea or not. The decisions are made at several stages in the innovation process, as demonstrated in the earlier funnel model.

Innovation department

An innovation department also functions as a control mechanism. It sorts the ideas, and those the department finds to be in accordance with the strategy are presented to the top management for a decision on whether to go further.

An innovation department can be an effective balancing factor if it functions efficiently.

Top entrepreneur

The existence of the top entrepreneur also functions as a control mechanism. He is so dominant that most new ideas are created 'in his own image'. Not many innovations outside this are accepted. His way of thinking is both an inspiration to and a limitation on innovation activities.

The danger is that all innovation capacity is bound up with this top entrepreneur. If he fails, everything goes wrong. This happened in two firms in my case studies. Both lost a great deal of money because of this type of entrepreneurship, and one of them, an insurance company, has since gone bankrupt. The problem was who should control the top manager. Some of the top entrepreneur's ideas were catastrophic failures. The employees and other managers in the two firms spent much time sorting out the most unrealistic of the top entrepreneur's ideas, but they were not able to discard all of them.

Organizational learning

Perhaps the most efficient, but also the most difficult, way to balance empowerment is through organizational learning (cf. Argyris and Schön 1978; Senge 1995). If the organization and its managers are able to learn continuously from mistakes and successes, and change the innovation organization and empowerment system accordingly, the firm has a chance of developing a better innovation capability.

Since innovation and empowerment are such complex and insecure processes, this may be the best control mechanism. It can help the organization to adapt to changes in its environment. It can also help to build up experience which tells the organization how efficient the various innovation resources are and which activities involve most risk.

The conclusion of my case studies was that the most efficient balancing of empowerment is obtained by having an institutionalized learning process and a certain degree of free intrapreneurship. Learning can be institutionalized by having methods or functions to collect and systematize experience and using them to change the intrapreneurship organizational system (like the linear phase model introduced in Chapter 11). However, innovation can probably never be a completely rational process, so a certain amount of free intrapreneurship which is not guided by former experience is needed. One aspect of learning is to gain experience of how much free intrapreneurship should be allowed in different situations.

None of the firms in the case studies I made had a perfect learning system. I will come back to the learning system in Chapter 15.

1.4.3 A Model for Balancing

The issue dealt with here has been how empowerment is balanced, that is, stimulated and controlled.

The interaction between the loosely coupled interaction system and the managerial structure is summarized in Figure 12.2. This is in fact a model of the 'stock' (the resources), the capabilities and the innovation management (cf. the model launched in Figure 9.1).

Figure 12.2   Model for balancing capabilities and resources

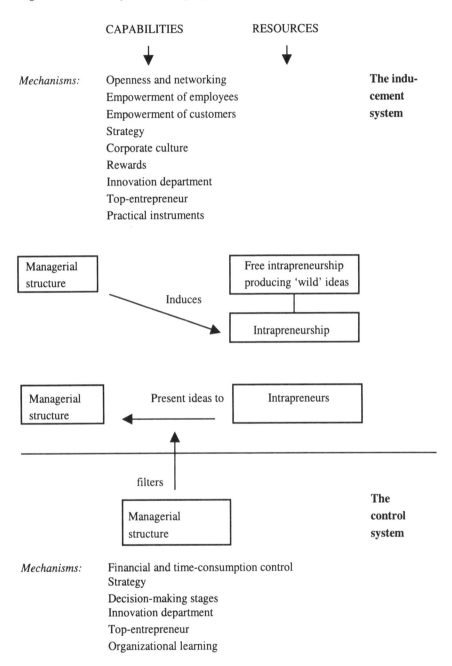

How empowerment is or should be balanced between inducement and control depends on two factors. One is the position of the enterprise in the innovation cycle (cf. Chapter 10) – whether it is in a recovery phase that requires innovations or in a phase where the market for current products is growing by itself. The other is the chosen strategy – whether it is a permanent, offensive, product-differentiation strategy, a productivity-maximizing strategy, or a more passive adaptation strategy.

Different mechanisms are used for improving innovation capability and balancing empowerment. Most of them are not strictly rational mechanisms in the sense that the effort and effect can be measured quantitatively. They are 'softer' or 'qualitative' behaviour-regulating mechanisms such as strategy, the decision-making path in the innovation process, organizational learning and so on. There is no rational economic resource allocation model that can solve the problem of balancing empowerment – at least not for the time being – and there probably never will be. A certain degree of economic control and, even better, time measurement, can supplement the other mechanisms.

The resources (the stock) are latent in intrapreneurs and their behaviour. The capabilities are the mechanisms and constitute the management's inducement and filtering activities. Innovation management is carried out through the managerial structure.

1.5 Power, Harmony and Conflict

Innovation is not only the rational creation of growth and benefits, it is also a social process involving power and conflict. Innovations are used by some groups or individuals to get more power in the organization, if they have the honour of being those who introduced the innovation. This increases their prestige and may be a basis for promotion and future power. This can be the case with the intrapreneur or with managers who make the innovation their project (even if they are not the creators of the idea). Innovations may be created in harmony or amidst conflict.

Mostly they are created in harmony (cf. the results of my case studies). This means that there is no open conflict and that the two structures, the managerial and the loosely coupled interactive one, agree.

Harmony may be active: both structures in the dual innovation organization actively promote innovation. The management has an active innovation-promoting policy that has been accepted by the employees. All or most employees and managers work actively to promote innovations. This means that there must be creativity and intrapreneurship within the firm and that the management must be open to new ideas and willing to accept failures (since many innovations fail). Employees must also be open to change and able to accept failures.

Harmony can also be passive: the management is innovation-oriented, but does not accept initiatives from below that it has not ordered. The loosely coupled innovation structure then becomes passive.

There may, however, be conflict. The social life of the firm – the loosely coupled interactive structure – produces ideas for innovations and entrepreneurship. However, it also produces counter-innovative forces: resistance to innovation, power systems and conflicts. The managerial structure is also involved in the power conflicts.

As part of the innovation process, the idea-creator, if he is an intrapreneur, must fight to get the idea accepted. He has various ways of waging a political struggle against the management. The intrapreneur can, for example, form an alliance with a customer or supplier, or he can form internal alliances. The idea-creator may also fight alone all the way and become a real intrapreneur, and this may create conflicts.

Finally there can be conflict over the idea in the loosely coupled interactive structure. I am not talking about the situation where the managerial structure has accepted or rejected the idea, but the situation before that when the management has not yet decided anything finally.

In the preliminary stage, the following general types of power manifestations and conflicts may appear.

1. Hierarchical struggles. Some middle or top managers (but not the whole top management) manifest their power by arousing hostility to the idea. This is irrational behaviour in relation to innovation because it may stop ideas that could be developed into innovations which are useful to the firm. However, the idea may not be considered useful to the careers of these managers.
2. Reward struggles. If there is a prospect of a reward, employees or managers may attempt to take the credit for the idea to get the reward themselves. This can create a struggle that will stop the innovation process.
3. Institutional struggles. A department may reject the innovation simply because it has been generated in another department, or it may try to take over the innovation. In these institutional power manifestations, people can take over roles from one another. For example, the problem-solving role may be taken over from the person who first discovered the problem and given either to another individual or to a group.

If the idea survives these power struggles in the first phase, it has a good chance of being developed into an innovation project, even if a struggle arises over it. Then the whole matter becomes an important discourse (cf. Foucault

1980) – there will be a strong focus on it. It may also fail: (1) if the idea-creator does not have the energy or ability to continue fighting for it; (2) if there is no prospect of a reward; (3) if the collective resistance is too great; and (4) if the resistance from the closest manager is too strong.

In such struggles people refer to the strategy or the current management policy of the firm, because these represent authority.

The power process is even more complex, since there are actors other than the dual organizational structure, namely the external ones: the owners (or shareholders), suppliers, customers, government authorities and so on. These actors are mostly external, but shareholders may be considered internal. They may have an active interest in innovations being made, or in them not being made. They can be enemies of the intrapreneurs or of the top management that wants to promote a certain innovation. They may, on the other hand, also be used by groups or individuals in the organization as allies, to promote the interests of these groups or individuals.

The external actors may also have conflicting interests, which makes the innovation process even more complicated. If this is the case with customer groups, and if the fulfilment of the needs of one customer group conflicts with the wishes of another (such as when a benefit for one group creates environmental problems), this creates a real dilemma for the firm.

2 MANAGEMENT INITIATION

The innovation process may also be run from the top. In this case I am not talking about the induced innovation discussed in the foregoing section, where the management creates incentives so that ideas can arise among the employees. Here I mean the situation where the top manager or group of top managers has the idea and wants it developed without involving the broader organization. In other words, I am talking about the first formulation of the idea (not its further development in the next phase). The idea may have come from outside the firm (from any of the external trajectories or actors) or the top manager may have had it himself. The point of departure is generally the strategy or management policy for development and innovation in the firm, but it may also be simply an isolated, 'wild' idea.

In this situation, only the hierarchical, managerial part of the dual organization (as described in the model in Chapter 10) is activated. This is a non-interactive process.

The task for the management is to establish rationally whether the firm has among its stock the resources necessary to develop the idea further. If it does not, it must acquire these from outside. The necessary resources may be, for example, capital – in which case the management may have to go to the financial market to get it. It may be specific competencies; if the firm does not have them, it must hire new people. Innovation management then rests with the top manager, who must acquire the right resources and organize the development of the idea (cf. the model in Chapter 9). The capabilities involved are the management's experience of organizing the development of ideas, of getting the right people so that the process can run smoothly (which requires competencies other than knowledge related to the idea).

How can this innovation management be done? Many ways can be found empirically. The one chosen depends on the capability of the manager in the firm in question. The experience and personal management styles of managers are different. From my research three general management styles can be identified:

1. *The top entrepreneur.* In cases where there is a top entrepreneur he can act in different ways; for example interactively, as described in the foregoing section – inspiring other people or carrying his own idea through, but remaining open to suggestions and objections. He can also act dictatorially – deciding simply to push his own idea through without listening to anyone else. He will often try to convince other people in the organization of the value of his idea, but he will not listen to objections, only to expressions of approval. In this case he works on his own to develop the idea and becomes a real entrepreneur: he is an intrapreneur who is in a power situation where he does not need to fight for his idea. He acts as if he owns the firm (and sometimes in fact he does). The dictatorial top entrepreneur may create much innovation, but he is also a risk. He can be a disaster for the firm because his idea are not discussed and tried out by other people.

2. *Establishment of a top-managed innovation department.* The top manager can establish an innovation department as a permanent service for the development of his ideas as a kind of staff function. This is neither the broad, idea-collecting department described in the foregoing section nor an R&D department. An R&D department is staffed by experts who are strong because of their professional background, and could oppose the top entrepreneur.

3. *Project teams.* The management can implement an innovation process immediately by setting up a structure to develop it. It may consist of just one person selected for the task. Some top managers pick such persons from the bottom of the organization and let them work directly under the top management outside the normal hierarchy. The management may also establish an idea project team; this is the normal approach. This group is given the task of developing the idea and is often placed directly under the top management.

This pure top-down initiation exists in many firms. However, one can argue that this situation is not the most efficient one, because the foundation for idea generation is too small compared with that of the dual organization. The risk of making mistakes can also be greater because the ideas are not discussed in a larger forum. One could argue that this could lead to more radical innovations. A collectivity such as an organization often has a tendency to be conservative and to reject radical ideas. However, in the dual organization too the management decides, and can decide to encourage and accept radical ideas.

In the case studies I have done, the pure top-down situation was not as common as the dual organization situation, although it did exist. Mostly it existed within the same firm, alternating with the dual organization situation. Thus the conclusion could be that the dual organization model can explain all the innovation processes, but sometimes only the managerial structure is activated – just as in other situations only the loosely coupled interactive structure is activated, as described in the foregoing section.

3 THE FORMAL KNOWLEDGE OR R&D APPROACH

This is an approach requiring experts. Although earlier I more or less defined the R&D approach as lying outside the strategic innovation theory, this is a case where the R&D system involves other parts of the firm in the innovation process. Generally, this is only used for technological innovations.

In this case the R&D department represents the innovative resources and the capabilities (through its tradition of conducting research). Innovation is also managed by this department, but with the top management ultimately deciding on the important steps.

The innovation process may start in two ways. One is when the problems have been defined and must be solved. Management establishes project teams or a permanent R&D department to conduct research in order to develop innovations that can solve the problems. The other is when new ideas come from outside, that is new technology or research results which can form the basis for innovations even if no problem has been defined. This requires considerable prior knowledge and great attention to external knowledge channels. This attention may either be individual and professional (a group of professionals follows the developments in their profession) or organized (for example, an R&D department has the responsibility).

The ideas from outside often follow a technological trajectory (cf. Dosi 1982). The professionals who staff the R&D functions are disciplined innovators who follow the traditions and trajectories of their profession.

There may be R&D functions or departments established on the basis of the service professions (for example, insurance professionals, management consultants, cleaning as a profession and so on). The innovations will then generally follow service profession trajectories (with the norms, problems and theories that the profession in question works with) (Sundbo and Gallouj 2000).

The different trajectories may replace one another (for example, a mechanical tradition with an information technology tradition, or a technological with a service profession trajectory).

The R&D department or other established organization cannot limit its activities to research. Some intrapreneurship (promotion and struggle to get the innovation accepted) is needed for the innovation to be accepted and successfully implemented in the organization. This function may be left to another part of the organization, but to avoid potential conflict and resistance to innovations, it is best if the R&D department itself plays this role. The innovation may also be developed in a social structure of professionals.

This is a burdensome approach because it requires much knowledge and thus many professionals. The use of information and communication technology as a channel for providing information and knowledge is important here.

It is an advantage if the R&D function cooperates with the marketing function, in particular when ideas are selected for further development. The strategy can form a point of reference in the selection process.

Top management intervenes in the process by defining which problems should be on the agenda. The management also decides how much the firm should invest in R&D activities. This decision should follow the innovation cycle if it is efficient.

Conflicts can also arise from this method of innovating. The experts may disagree, or there may be a conflict between them and the management. The professionals follow two goals: one is to serve the interests of the firm, and the other is to adhere to the norms and paradigms of the profession. This may produce conflicts between the professionals and the top management. The possibility of replacing one trajectory with another may also produce conflicts among the professionals themselves.

The formal organization of responsibility and knowledge gate-keeping represented by this approach may be an advantage, even for service firms. It exists in many, though far from all, manufacturing firms, but in very few service firms (Sundbo 1998a, Sundbo and Gallouj 2000). However, it can be argued that it is most efficient when associated with the dual innovation organization type. The formal system or R&D department can then interact with and exploit the loosely coupled interactive structure – both because there can be much creativity, intrapreneurship and knowledge in that structure, and because this can prevent conflict and resistance.

13. The Development Phase

This chapter deals with the second phase of the innovation process. It will discuss different aspects of the behaviour of firms and individuals, and the organization of this phase. The development phase is the process where the idea (or invention) is developed into a prototype or completed plan (for example, for an organizational change or a new kind of market behaviour). Now we go from the more anarchistic creative situation that characterized the initialization phase to a more organized situation.

First, I will state the general principles for understanding the development process.

1 GENERAL PRINCIPLES FOR UNDERSTANDING THE DEVELOPMENT PROCESS

I have already introduced a principle of duality or balance as a basis for understanding innovation. The dual organization and balancing of the intrapreneurship activities were discussed in the foregoing chapters. This principle will also be invoked in the discussion of the development phase.

In the history of innovation theory, several unidimensional explanations of the innovation process have been proposed. Two of these in particular should be mentioned. One is the entrepreneur theory's emphasis on creativity and norm-breaking behaviour (cf. Sexton and Schön 1986; Sexton and Kasarda 1992). Within the framework of the strategic innovation theory, this is too individualistic an explanation. As stated before, the innovation process must be considered as something organized and collective, involving a management. Modern economics has emphasized institutionalization (see, for example, Hodgson 1988) and this has also to some extent been applied to innovation, for example in the theory of innovation systems and path-dependency (for example, Eliasson 1989).

This explanation suggests that the firm follows certain external trajectories in its innovation activities, but that the 'path' also includes the internal way of thinking about and organizing innovation, and relations with the same external actors. The innovations in the individual firm are – at least to some degree – determined by an institutionalized innovation system in society (for example, traditions of research, knowledge diffusion and so on) and by institutionalized forms of innovation behaviour within the firm itself. This theory is empirically based. However, the results of my own and others' empirical studies show that there may be some institutionalization of the innovation process, but that it is also characterized by path-breaking, norm-breaking and anarchistic behaviour. These are phenomena that characterize entrepreneurship. The innovation process thus cannot be understood solely from an institutional perspective.

The approach applied here will fundamentally involve a dual and balancing perspective. We need to state the principles for two aspects of the development process: (1) what is the driving force of the process, and (2) how is the process organized? These will be the main questions to answer in this chapter.

2 THE DRIVING FORCE OF THE DEVELOPMENT PROCESS

As the discussion in the foregoing section has shown, the development process can be considered as having two opposite driving forces: an institutionalizing one and a path-breaking one.

The institutional driving force is the tendency to institutionalize behaviour related to innovation processes in fixed patterns, with certain norms, ways of finding knowledge, procedures for activities and so on. The innovation process becomes path-dependent, which means that it follows certain external trajectories. Institutionalization as a sociological concept does not mean that patterns are decreed from above. These may exist in very rare cases, but generally they are developed from below. The development of institutional patterns can be explained as en expression of the conservative nature of man. Social beings look for safety. If procedures are known, people are better able to predict what will happen if they act in a certain way or offer a certain opinion. This factor even influences innovation processes, which are not only processes of maximal change, but also ways of gaining power and social prestige. Rationally, one can explain institutionalization as a learning process: when people perceive that a certain kind of behaviour leads to a good result, they tend to repeat that kind of behaviour. And the same applies to innovation.

Path-breaking behaviour involves looking for new paths, and this will often infringe the norms and usual patterns of behaviour. It may also break with the usual pattern of thinking and knowledge and thus with the existing trajectories. This is related to the orientation towards creativity and action that characterizes entrepreneurs, and can be explained sociologically by the fact that mankind also has a drive to explore and to make things better. But this drive is less general; if it were universal there would be no patterns, no institutions and no sociology. Some individuals have this drive, and they create or start processes of change (cf. Tarde 1895). Rationally, this may be explained in terms of the need to find new solutions, new ways of doing things, which means not only taking new steps on the established road, but also establishing of new roads.

Since both tendencies exist and are important to the development process, the process can be considered as driven by the balance between institutionalization and path-breaking. This balance can be assumed to be different in different situations. One would expect it to depend on where in the innovation cycle a firm is: path-breaking can be assumed to be most important at the end of the 'turn' phase (cf. the model of strategic phases in Chapter 10) while institutionalization becomes most important in the growth phase.

A downturn in a curve requires radical solutions (path-breaking), and when solutions have been found it is important to maintain the progress made through institutionalization.

Different types of firm can also have a different balance. In Figure 13.1 is a theoretical model of this (based on, among other things, my case studies in the service sector).

Figure 13.1   Balance of institutionalization and path-breaking

	Much institutionalization	**Little institutionalization**
Much path breaking	*Hyper innovative firms* (exploit all existing channels and are radical path-breaking as well)	*Entrepreneur firms* (focused on path-breaking)
Little path breaking	*Mature firms* (but of the innovating kind)	*Innovative newcomers* (neither very path-breaking, nor with much tradition for innovation)

3   THE FORMS OF INNOVATION

3.1   Different Types of Innovation

Do different types of innovation have different courses of development?

One dimension involves the following types of innovation: product, process, organizational, market and raw materials. Their development processes differ, as will be reflected in section 5. Often these types will be integrated; this was typical in the service firms I studied, for example, because a new product required a new kind of organization, a new process and new market behaviour.

Another dimension involves manufacturing (goods or physical) versus service innovations. These are generally similar in their course of development (Sundbo 1998a, Sundbo and Gallouj 1999). There are some differences when it comes to product (goods or services), process and raw material innovations, but these are not organizational and market differences. In manufacturing the development of new goods is more often placed in an R&D department and more influenced by the technical world outside the firm. The latter is also typical of process and raw material innovations in manufacturing. Service innovations are more internally developed, with less use of formal R&D departments and external formal knowledge trajectories (cf. my case studies).

A third dimension involves technological and non-technological innovations. Their development is often similar, but the development of technological innovations is more related to (or takes place in) an R&D department or an information and communication technology department, and is more influenced by the technical world outside the firm.

Where differences are thought to be evident, they will be emphasized in this chapter, but otherwise the development of manufacturing and services, and of technological and non-technological innovations, will be treated in the same way.

3.2 Differentiated Standardization

One particular development of the forms of innovation is differentiated standardization. This is the tendency to procure individual commodities and services for customers while still maintaining the cost reduction that standardized production permits. This principle is also implemented in marketing, where the 'personal relationship' marketing that characterizes services (Gummesson 1999) is generalized. This principle has also been called flexible specialization (Piore and Sabel 1984, Volberda 1998), mass customization (Pine 1993) and modularization (Sundbo 1994); other terms have also been used.

Differentiated standardization is a combination of the standardization known from mass production manufacturing and the individual customer care known from traditional service production (see, for example, Eiglier and Langeard 1988); it attempts to combine the advantages of both. This is done, among other ways, by increasingly combining commodities with services.

This principle has been observed in practice in both manufacturing (Pine 1993) and services (Sundbo 1998a) and it may now be taken to be part the contemporary development of most firms. It is therefore posited in the strategic innovation theory that in their development process firms will attempt to realize the principle of differentiated standardization.

3.3   Technology as an Open Question

Which technological form a product and process innovation should take is another open question that must be adressed throughout the development process. In services, the question is often whether the innovation should be given a technological form or should be manual. For example, should information and communication technology be used? A new banking service could be offered by the personnel in a bank branch or could be produced by the customers themselves on a machine as self-service. More manual services, such as cleaning, hotel work and restaurants could be produced by using technology (for example, automats) or by using personnel. Even in manufacturing it is often an open question which technique should be used. Different materials – metal, plastic and so on – can be used to achieve the same result. This is also an issue in most development processes.

4   RESOURCES AND CAPABILITIES

Resources and capabilities are also core factors in the development phase. The other two core factors, trajectories and external actors, will be dealt with later.

The development process depends on the resources that the firm has or can procure and on its capabilities, that is, its ability to mobilize the right resources. The innovation capability depends mostly on the managerial structure, but the loosely coupled interactive structure still plays a role (although less so than in the initialization phase, because the development phase is more organized). Resource activation or procurement requires the action and interaction of employees and middle managers. It was demonstrated earlier that this is a characteristic of an innovative organization (see, for example, Burns and Stalker 1961; Nyström 1979).

The resources needed for development can be of many kinds, depending on the innovations in question. No general picture can be given of this; we can only list the most important factors. They are:

- Knowledge
- Capital
- Ability to organize (management resource)
- Formal organization (for example, the existence of an R&D department)
- Employee motivation to participate in development activities
- Relations and alliances with external actors
- Technology

The most crucial factor is the ability to activate and procure the right resources at the right time (cf. the cyclical model of the strategy situation of the firm). Not only should the right resources be activated, they should be activated in the optimal proportions. Too little is insufficient to develop the innovation, too much is a waste of resources. The capabilities for development are primarily a matter for the management, but the loosely coupled interactive structure is also important for some capabilities. Activation of resources in an organization also requires that the employees act and interact, for example to develop new company-internal knowledge that does not yet exist.

The required development capabilities can be of many kinds depending on the situation, but generally the following are among the most crucial:

- Involving and procuring the right resources in the right proportions
  This depends on the managerial and the loosely coupled interactive structures
- Making the right decisions in relation to future market possibilities
  This depends on the managerial structure
- Creating an efficient formal organization
  This depends on the managerial structure
- Creating a fruitful interaction process which does not run out of control in the loosely coupled interactive structure
  This depends on the managerial and the loosely coupled interactive structures and on the interaction between the two structures
- Involving external trajectories and actors
  This depends on the managerial and loosely coupled interactive structures

If the firm does not have the appropriate resources, it can attempt to buy them on the market or procure them externally or internally in other ways. If it does not have the appropriate capabilities, it is more difficult. The capabilities that are situated in the loosely coupled interactive structure are extremely difficult to change. This is only possible over a long space of time, if at all. A firm cannot just replace all its employees. A new interaction structure and corporate culture must also emerge. The only factor that can be changed in the short run is the managerial structure. Even though this too involves certain patterns of interaction among managers, norms and cultural values, it is easier to replace the managers with other types. However, this will generally not be done unless the goal is a radical innovation that can change the product and production profile totally, or unless the lack of development capability proves to be permanent.

5 ORGANIZATION OF THE DEVELOPMENT ACTIVITIES

5.1 Development as a Sociological Process in General

The development process is more institutionalized and more guided by the managerial structure than the initialization phase. There are only a few possibilities for the loosely coupled interactive structure. The ability to organize becomes more crucial, as does the management's ability to decide whether an idea will be successful or not. Decision-making becomes more crucial than creativity.

The roles of the employees are changed. There is little room for free intrapreneurship. The intrapreneur must struggle extremely hard if he wants to retain ownership of the innovation and carry out the development himself. He will normally be a member of the project team that is to develop the innovation, but this will be a different role – a disciplined working role in a hierarchical structure (although the project team hierarchy is often rather loose). The roles are no longer free and it is difficult to carve out one's own role, since the roles are generally ascribed. Management often puts individual employees and managers in a project team because they are supposed to play a certain role.

This means that the norms, values and behavioural patterns of the loosely coupled interactive structure are transferred to the development organization, but in a more structured and guided way than in the initialization phase.

5.2 Formal Organization

The development phase can be organized in different ways, depending among other things on whether the innovation is a radical, large-scale, reproduced one or a minor incremental, ad hoc innovation. It also differs from enterprise to enterprise, depending on traditions, culture, the managers' ideas etc. Some firms do have an R&D department (or just a development department), some do not.

Furthermore, the formal organization is different for different types of innovation – product, process, market innovation and so on. The organization of the development process must therefore be treated differently according to the innovation type, and this will be discussed in this section.

Product development
The development phase can be organized in two ways:

1. *In the R&D department.* This could be a kind of 'normal' production in the R&D department. Either one or a few persons are given certain tasks and the

development process is coordinated by a manager in the R&D department; or the development can be organized by a project team within the R&D department. Often the project team is expanded using people from other parts of the organization. This is advisable if one want the innovation to be a success (Tidd, Bessant and Pavitt 1997).

2. *In a cross-departmental project team.* This is becoming increasingly frequent, even when the firm has an R&D department. It differs from the situation described above insofar as the R&D department is not actually managing the development work. This may be done by a manager from a production department, from the top management's office (often from the strategy group) or, very often, from the marketing department. The R&D department then functions as a specialized service unit (cf. Mattsson 1994). The R&D department can be assumed to have a stronger position the more high-tech the industry. However, often the firms do not have an R&D department.

Cross-departmental project teams can be assumed to be the normal way of organizing the development activities in firms for which the strategic innovation theory is valid (this was the case in service firms and it is becoming increasingly popular in manufacturing firms – cf. Cooper 1988). The reason is that many factors are important in development, not least whether the new product can be sold on the market. Normally a project manager will be nominated, either a manager or an employee. The team members will be given different roles; some of these roles will be ascribed (as mentioned before); others will develop during the process, either out of necessity or because the team members develop their roles themselves. These roles are related to the group process. For example, there may be the role of always asking critical questions, the creative role, the knowledge procurement role, and the knowledge-synthesizing role, as well as the conflict-resolving role.

The case studies in services showed that future managers often emerge from these team-oriented development processes. They may be the former intrapreneurs, or new people who demonstrate management abilities in this phase. Often they start by leading a group that is to implement the innovation, and later become managers elsewhere in the organization.

A development project involves the collection of knowledge, creativity and the disciplining of the group members. The process can be and often is complex and unpredictable (Kline 1985). Project management becomes an important discipline. The project manager must not only be able to procure the right knowledge and technical solutions, he or she must also be able to make the project members cooperate. Often he must also be able to manage the use of information and communication technology as a development instrument. Intrapreneurship must be even more tied here (Sundbo 1992a). If there is a top intrapreneur, he or she will in most cases follow the process very closely.

The success factors in project team work are:

- Time efficiency – the ability to handle complex and unpredictable tasks relatively fast
- Knowledge procurement ability
- The development of different roles in the project process such as:
  - the problem finder   (asks questions)
  - the problemsolver
  - the coordinator
  - the actor
- Good project management ('coaching', taking initiatives)
- Free frameworks for the content of the work
- - but fixed frameworks for goals and time limits
- Quality control
- Learning that is passed on to the next teams
- Use of information and communication technology as an instrument for development

Development of process and organizational innovations

The development of these innovations is often organized in project teams, as described above. The difference is that the production departments play a leading role in process innovations. In organizational innovations the production department or the personnel department plays the leading role; so may the top management if a comprehensive organizational change is to be made or if there is the potential for conflict between employees and the firm. Which department plays the leading role also depends on the internal power situation in the organization.

A production department sometimes carries out the development by itself (if it is a minor innovation). In some situations the personnel department may carry out an organizational development on its own, but it needs to interact with many internal actors, departments as well as personnel groups, and the top management.

In the process of developing organizational innovations, the management will generally involve the employees and middle managers. This is a precondition for successful implementation. The involvement can be organized in several ways: as a broad information and discussion process; by involving employees in the project teams; by negotiating with the shop stewards; or otherwise.

The only cases I have found where the process has run smoothly without this type of involvement are the rare situations where the top manager has definite charisma. In all these cases he was a top entrepreneur and could manage the development process in a purely top-down fashion.

Development of the use of a new raw material or other supplies
This can be organized in the same way as product development. However, often a production department carries out this type of innovation, particularly if it is a minor one. A production department has the necessary relationship with suppliers and follows new developments in supply materials.

Development of market innovations
The development can be organized in a cross-departmental project team. The marketing department will normally lead this process. The development can also take place within the marketing department, either organized in a project team or simply using the normal division of labour, with single individuals responsible for parts of the development.

5.3 Roles

Although the development process is more organized than the initialization phase, there will still be roles. These will be more of the ascribed type, as mentioned before, with more orientation towards team-building and team processes. The self-centred, on-rushing intrapreneur role becomes rarer, and social roles become more frequent and more differentiated, representing different functions in the team process, as described above.

In my studies of innovation in service firms I defined three main roles: (1) the intrapreneur; (2) the analyst, who is occupied with procuring knowledge and analysing the situation; and (3) the producer, who is occupied with his daily job routines (whatever they may be). In the development phase the analyst takes on the most important role. Only when the problems cannot be solved within existing knowledge trajectories does the intrapreneur come into focus again.

5.4 The Social Process – Power and Conflicts

Power plays and conflicts are not conspicuous in this phase – at least as far as my studies of service firms show (Sundbo 1998a). Nevertheless they do exist. Different departments may fight for the right to be the developer, and there may be struggles over which department is to produce the product in future or manage the process or organizational change.

The level at which there is most conflict in this phase is that of the individual. Individuals position themselves in relation to the possible advantages that the innovation could give them in the future, as my case studies have demonstrated (cf. Chapter 15). The advantage may be promotion, a better working situation, increased salary and so on. In particular, the originators of the idea and the members of project teams outside an R&D or innovation department take up their positions. Conflicts are, however, rarely open. That would be too risky and could destroy one's position in the internal competition. They are mostly hidden, but that makes it more difficult to resolve them and complicates the decision as to whether to go on with the innovation. It makes it difficult for the managerial structure to assess how well the social and organizational process is going.

Another problem at the individual level is whether the employees can be motivated to participate in project teams, which often require great effort and sometimes take up employees' leisure time. This depends on the extended bargaining (cf. Sundbo 1999): employees are willing to make this sacrifice if they get some reward.

6 THE DECISION-MAKING SYSTEM

As mentioned before, decisions are very important in this phase. In this section I will discuss the nature of the decision-making system.

6.1 The Formal Decision-Making System

The managerial structure is the formal decision-making system. Top management makes the principal decisions. These are of two kinds: first, the decision as to whether to develop an idea into an innovation; and second, the decision, at different stages of the process, as towhether or not to go on with the development.

The decision-making process can be described by a model, the 'decision funnel', which was introduced in Chapter 12.

If it is decided to develop the idea, it becomes a 'project'. The goal of the development process is more clearly defined, although it can be changed during the process. The idea and the organizational structure necessary to implement it are identified. This does not necessarily mean that the project is highly formalized, but at all events the innovation process will not be as fluid as during the initialization phase. Both large-scale and small-scale reproduced innovations are possible. The development of the former is more often organized as an identifiable project with a formal structure. The development of the latter is sometimes organized in the same way, but at other times is more informal and no project team is established. The development can, for example, be carried out in a product department as part of its normal work. In this case, the development process cannot be separated from daily production work.

Decision-making along the way is necessary because most innovation attempts fail, so it is rational to stop projects that will fail – the sooner the better. Of course the problem is knowing which projects will fail. The likelihood of success or failure can be established on the basis of experience of similar projects and situations, but each innovation has its own life and the outcome cannot be predicted accurately. Thus the ongoing decisions cannot be made rationally.

The general criteria for the decisions are:

1. the strategy;
2. the market potential; and
3. the technical and organizational potential for realizing the idea.

The strategy is the management's first framework for decision-making. The technical potential is the traditional innovation factor known from technology–economic innovation theory. It is supplemented by the social factor, the possibility of finding people with the competencies to develop the innovation and make it work in practice, and the possibility of organizing the work after the innovation has been implemented.

The market potential is the most important factor because it is the ultimate for success or failure. This factor dominates the other two in the decision-making process. This was the case in the service firms, where the development process was organized around this issue.

Other criteria are also used. In the first development period, the possible actions of the competitors play a major role, as do technical potential and the possibility of obtaining relevant knowledge. Management will often look at the firm's resources and capabilities in order to decide. In the later development period these factors still play a role, but the cost of the project is added as a decision-making factor, as is an evaluation of how the 'project' is functioning socially and organizationally. The resources and capabilities are constantly considered. Do we have the right resources? Can we get the resources we do not have, and what will they cost? Are we using our abilities optimally? Negative answers to these questions can lead to either a correction of the development process or its abandonment.

Other layers of management apart from top management are involved in the decision-making process. They are involved in the first decision – whether to start the development process at all; and they often make the ongoing decisions. Only the principal decisions are presented to top management during the development process. However, in the servcie firms I studied, the degree to which top management interfered in the details of daily development work differed among firms and depended on their management style. The marketing department and its managers often lead the process because of the primacy of market potential. This was clear in the service firms, while in manufacturing firms it is not so common (cf. Tidd, Bessant and Pavitt 1997). If the innovation involves much technology, in particular high-tech, the R&D department or the information and communication technology department may take the lead, but always with the marketing department as a strong co-player – or perhaps counterpart. The latter is the case even when the development is carried out by the R&D department alone.

6.2 Economy

In the development phase, economic factors become more of an issue. The initialization phase is diffuse and is difficult to account for in terms of money (and even time). The development phase is generally more organized, and the management attempts to maintain control of spending through tight organization and frequent assessments of whether each innovation project should continue. The assessment is based on two criteria: (1) the possible cost of the project; and (2) the potential income or savings.

One resource is capital. In this phase it is necessary to investigate whether capital can be raised for development and implementation. This requires powers of persuasion, even if the capital can be procured internally. It may be necessary to convince the board or shareholders. Persuasion is easier the more analyses one has of the market and competitors, and the more knowledge one has. It is also important for top management to prove that the innovation remains within the framework of the strategy. Analytical knowledge and proof that the innovation can be accommodated within a successful strategy will make it easier to procure capital outside the firm. Banks and other investors are often uncertain about how to assess innovation projects, and such information improves the potential for applying for capital.

Sometimes shareholders are most easily convinced if the firm strikes out on the innovation path, as demonstrated by the current increasing interest in shares in the most innovative and path-breaking information and communication technology firms.

7 EXTERNAL PARTNERS AND TRAJECTORIES

The trajectories and external actors with which the firm can collaborate become most important in the development phase. In this phase the idea is clear. The firm needs to collect knowledge and ideas, and must already begin to find the partners who will be necessary in the implementation and perhaps the later production phase.

This is a matter of external collaboration and networking. It has been emphasized and described much in recent literature (for example, Håkansson 1987; Piore and Sabel 1984; Nelson 1993).

Often firms will participate in external partnerships. These may be of a more permanent type, but are often loosely coupled networks (cf. Håkansson 1987) which are not institutionalized. This pattern is best analysed in terms of general sociological behaviour patterns – actions, interactions, 'friendships' and antagonisms among firms (in the same way as among individual group members). It will rarely be institutionalized because it changes frequently.

7.1 Trajectories

The trajectories included in the model given in Chapter 7 define the universe of external pressure to make changes and the paths for procuring knowledge. Sometimes firms want to follow a trajectory because it will lead them to knowledge (cf. Dosi 1982; Perez 1983). On the other hand they are bound by the trajectory (path-dependency), and brilliant solutions may lie outside the trajectory. The problem of following a trajectory is how the firm will differ from its competitors, who may also be assumed to be constantly looking for new solutions and innovations. Thus sometimes it is an advantage to break away from the trajectory, although this may be difficult because employees are bound by it. It can be done if one intrapreneur – or a group of intrapreneurs – breaks away from the trajectory and takes the innovation all the way (this comes from the loosely coupled interactive structure). It can also happen if one or more managers insist on breaking away from the trajectory. In this case they need to either do it themselves or find someone who can play the role of path-breaker and assign this role to him. Teams may also be path-breakers, although this is more difficult. A conservative inertia seems to be built into collectivities like teams. In my case studies, the most path-breaking teams were 'amateurs', that is non-experts, such as when a group of salespeople had a technical problem or a production team had a marketing problem. Such groups tend to be less bound by the professional or technological trajectories.

Which trajectories are used in development processes of course depends on the specific innovation and firm. The trajectories mentioned in Chapter 7 define the universe of pressure and knowledge as broad. This universe involves much more than the technological–scientific world and than the service trajectories.

Since the market potential in this theoretical framework is assumed to be more important than technological inventions and professional ideas, knowledge of the future market potential is the most important kind. This means that social and institutional trajectories are more important than technological and service profession trajectories when it comes to product and marketing innovations and innovations in raw materials. This is true even when it comes to process and organizational innovations, but in manufacturing managerial and technological trajectories may be just as important because customers do not see the processes and the organization (as they do in services). However, the more manufacturing becomes politicized – as customers become interested in environmental problems and working conditions – the more the social and institutional trajectories become the important ones even there.

7.2 Actors

External actors will often be involved in the development process because:

- knowledge is difficult to obtain and external actors possess knowledge;
- the development process requires much effort as regards not only knowledge, but also capital, technology and other resources that external actors possess;
- society influences the sales prospects; this is the case with potential customers, but also with unions, trade associations, governments and others who regulate trade and industry; and
- some suppliers (such as consultants) can be used by management to guide the development process (that is, for power purposes).

The service cases showed that if the innovations are too easy to imitate (which is often the case in services because products, processes and so on are simple), this is an impediment to external collaboration and networking.

All the actors mentioned in the model are relevant, and which ones will be involved depends on the concrete situation. In all situations the customers are crucial actors, and if a product or market innovation is the aim, the development process will be better if they are involved. They can be involved as partners in the whole development process, which is often the case if the firm sells its products to other firms. Whatever the case, it will increase the chance of success in product innovation if a prototype is tested on a customer panel, and this will often be done. A surprising result of my case studies was that service firms, which according to service management and marketing theory (Grönroos 1990; Normann 1991) are particularly customer-oriented, often had difficulty in involving customers significantly in the development process. Often it was only in the late phase, when a prototype of the innovation was tested, that customers became really involved.

8 INTERNATIONALIZATION

The development process has become more international because of three factors. One is that markets and market competition have become more international. The second is that firms therefore become multinational. The third is that the necessary knowledge must very often be collected from sources in many countries. The external actors also become more international. A factor such as the development of the internet (and other kinds of international information and communication networks) will increase this tendency. Some of my investigations demonstrated that service firms become more innovative the more international competition they have (SIC 1999).

The innovation must compete on a global market. Even such geographically bound activities as cleaning and the care sector (for example, care of the elderly), which must be done in customers' homes by local staff, are exposed to international competition. Foreign companies buy local ones if the latter are not efficient. This is reflected in firms' strategies and the development process must take it into account. If the process is to be efficient, all potential knowledge bases must be utilized, including foreign ones.

This is why the notion of a national system of innovation is no longer adequate. Various other types of system certainly exist (although they are generally rather loosely coupled systems), but they can rarely be considered particularly national in their limitations. They can be global or work in a field that is narrower than the nation.

There is a wide range of forms of internationalization in the development phase, for example:

- the firm is international and the development process involves cooperation among departments in different countries
- knowledge is collected from international sources
- the firm has alliances and cooperates with similar firms in other countries (which could be potential competitors)
- global market analyses can guide the development process
- international financing can be raised for the development process
- the firm may place its development project in another country; it may, for example, buy it as a service from a foreign R&D company or its own R&D department may be located in a 'knowledge district' (such as Silicon Valley) in another country.

14.   The Implementation Phase

In the last phase of the innovation process the innovation must be implemented, which means that it will begin to be used in practice. In this phase the functional problems are solved – except perhaps for some minor adjustments that prove necessary in the first period of use. The problems of knowledge and creativity are no longer at the top of the agenda. The problems that arise in this phase are related to the users' acceptance of the innovation. Overcoming these requires the ability to guide a social process (or a marketing process, which is also a social process), and this becomes the most important innovation capability during this stage.

1 THE PROBLEMS AND THE CAPABILITIES NEEDED

The task in the implementation phase is to 'sell' the innovation to the users, whether customers or employees, and to external actors who could impede the implementation (for example, political authorities). The marketing of the innovation becomes the crucial activity. The interaction pattern also changes. The crucial relationship is no longer that between the management and the employees in the loosely coupled interaction system, but that between the firm and the users. The latter may be customers, but they may also be the employees (for example if the innovation is organizational). However, they will often be employees other than those engaged in the innovation activities in the loosely coupled interactive structure. It is also crucial to get the market to accept the innovation, whichever type it is.

The ability to 'sell' the innovation becomes the most important resource and activating this ability becomes the most important priority.

To improve the implementation process, firms often test a prototype of the innovation on a user panel. If it is a product innovation, they use a customer panel (as was usual in the service firms I studied); if it is an organizational innovation, they start by introducing the new organization in a small part of the firm. This way they can learn, and adjust the innovation and the implementation process.

The problems of putting the innovation into production also demand specific skills (or resources), and the ability to organize production becomes a crucial innovation capability. By 'production' I mean producing a new commodity or service product if it is a product innovation, but also, for example, organizing new market behaviour for all relevant employees and managers if it is a market innovation.

2 DIFFERENT TYPES OF INNOVATION

The implementation process can be different for the different types of innovation. The innovation types can be viewed on a scale, with the implementation process ranging from a comprehensive internal social process, to an expert implementation process, to an externally directed marketing process. Furthermore, the implementation of a new element can lead to discussion in the press, intervention from regulating authorities and other processes in society which must be taken into account. The scale is expressed in Figure 14.1.

Figure 14.1   Innovation types

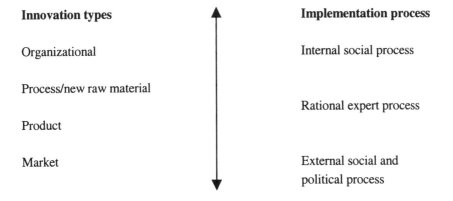

Innovation types	**Implementation process**
Organizational	Internal social process
Process/new raw material	
	Rational expert process
Product	
Market	External social and political process

3 IMPLEMENTATION AS A SOCIAL PROCESS: RESISTANCE, CONFLICT AND POWER STRUGGLES

The implementation process is a social and political process that could lead to the failure of the innovation. It is important to avoid the negative type of 'selling' where the firm arouses resistance to the innovation.

The success or failure of an innovation process is not only a rational matter – whether the users find it useful or not – even though the management attempts to handle it as such. It is also influenced by resistance, which has nothing to do with the rational aspects, from various internal and external actors. Power struggles and general conflicts that have nothing to do with the innovation may influence the process.

Internal conditions in the loosely coupled interactive structure and conflicts between employees and the top management may interfere with the process – more so the more we come to the top part of the model shown in Figure 14.1. This means that the interaction between the managerial and the loosely coupled interactive structure must be free of conflict and that the creation of new norms, behaviour and values in the loosely coupled interactive structure must support the implementation. This in turn requires that top management – or the part of the managerial structure entrusted with the implementation – prepare the employees for the innovation and ensure that there is no resistance from them. In the best case the employees will actively support the innovation without involving other interests or engaging in power struggles. Resistance from employees may be particularly strong if the innovation is organizational.

There may also be resistance and conflict from external actors. The market may not accept the innovation. This may be the classic case where potential customers do not buy a new product. However, the rise of the political and ethical consumer may cause negative market reactions to the firm even when an innovation is internal, such as a process or an organizational innovation or a market innovation. Regulating authorities may intervene. The latter case can to a certain extent be foreseen and the firm can ask the authorities whether the innovation will lead to any regulatory intervention. It is worse if consumer groups react. This is why the firm should ride on social trajectory waves rather than swim against them. Shareholders may also react negatively. The press may criticize the innovation or communicate rejection by other actors to the public and the political arena.

If the firm has other firms (competitors or not) as partners in the innovation process, there may also be conflicts among the partners. This could stop the innovation, or the other firms may 'run away with it'. Trust is crucial in innovative relationships. The best way to establish trust is by establishing long-lasting relationships and behave properly in these relationships. Legal contracts may also be useful, but they suffer from the disadvantage that it is difficult to specify problems in an innovation process legally. One never knows what problems will come up.

4 DECISIONS

In this phase there is only one decision for top management to make, namely whether the final implementation should be started or not. Once it is started, the management's role is simply to continue with the process and support it as well as it can. The decisions have already been made in relation to the strategy, so the decision criteria will come from the management's assessment of the prospects of success for the innovation within the chosen strategic framework – whether market success or successful internal implementation (if it is a process or organizational innovation).

Unusual and unforeseen situations can arise, and then it may be necessary to shut down the implementation process before it has been completed, but this will be rare. Such situations mainly arise if the innovation creates resistance and much internal or external discussion.

The implementation process includes the first period of the use of the innovation. Far from all innovations work well in practice. A new product may not sell very well, or it may not work perfectly. Problems may appear when a new process has been implemented, even if a prototype has been tested successfully. Such situations put pressure on the management regarding whether to remove the innovation again (if that is possible) or to make corrections. The latter course could lead to new projects and a series of new development and implementation processes.

In some of the service firms I have studied, the implementation phase was long and complicated because things did not work. For example a bank launched a new self-service banking product, there were failures caused by the information and communication technology supplier. In a catering firm launching a new canteen concept, employees needed a long time to get used to the new procedures.

If serious resistance and problems occur, this may lead to comprehensive and fundamental corrections. It may for example teach the management that the strategy is wrong, at least with respect to the situation into which the innovation process has led the firm. The strategy may be adjusted or completely reformulated.

The decisions in the implementation phase are clearly a management task and the managerial structure takes over here. The control of the implementation process becomes even more centralized and organized than is the case with the development process – it is left less to intrapreneurs.

5 ORGANIZATION OF THE IMPLEMENTATION PROCESS

The implementation process is more carefully planned than the foregoing processes. The management work is delegated by top management to the department that is to Administer the innovation in the future. This may be a production department if it is a product or process innovation or a new raw material, the marketing department if it is a market innovation, and any or all departments if it is an organizational innovation. The management changes from an innovation management to a production management. However, the marketing department (or a market-oriented function such as Public Relations) is deeply involved in the implementation since the market's acceptance of the innovation – of whatever type – is so important.

Different parts of the managerial structure can lead the implementation process. It may be assumed that it is in general led by the managers of the department that will administer the innovation, with the marketing managers acting as co-leaders.

Sometimes a new, permanent team or department will be established to administer the innovation: if it is a product innovation, this will be a new production department. In many of the service firms that I studied, a new team was set up with the most suitable members of the development team (who were far from always the intrapreneurs) as managers. If the product becomes a success, the team will be developed into a department. If it is a new process or organizational innovation, a team or department will manage the new process system or organizational effort (for example Quality Assurance or Business Process Reengineering) in the future. The new team or department will already have taken over the management of the implementation by this stage.

A temporary team may also carry out the implementation. Often the development project team itself will continue the work, but normally under close inspection by the managerial structure.

The loosely coupled interactive structure plays a less important role than in the first two phases. As an innovation-creating factor the loosely coupled interactive structure no longer has much of a function to fulfil. This is the case if the implementation process proceeds without problems.

One can assume that if there are still minor technical problems to solve, they will be solved by experts. However, if problems of a social nature occur, the loosely coupled interactive structure may be relevant in solving these problems.

6 PROTECTION AGAINST IMITATION

One problem in the implementation phase and shortly afterwards is protecting the innovation from imitation by competitors. I am not talking about competitors who may have been partners in the innovation process, but about other competitors who may have an interest in imitating the innovation. This could mean that the innovating firm cannot make all the potential profit and might perhaps not even recover its costs.

In manufacturing there have traditionally been means of protecting product innovations, primarily the patent system. For other types of innovation there are not many options. One could patent a process innovation (a method), but this is rather rare, and an organizational or market innovation cannot be patented. Furthermore, patenting does not always provide efficient protection because it takes a long time to get a patent and sometimes it is easy to get around the patent and introduce a nearly identical product without consequences. Thus the traditional patent system is not generally as efficient as has been assumed (Schmookler 1966).

In services, patents have been used very little, even to protect product innovations (SIC 1999). Service firms have used legal and social protection mechanisms such as intellectual property rights, or competition and customer clauses stipulating that employees are not allowed to take another job in the same industry or to work for the old firm's customers.

Service firms mainly use purely social protection mechanisms such as image and market position (SIC 1999). Even if another firm imitates the innovation, the firm that has introduced it will rely on its strong market position, hoping that customers will not buy the imitated service products. However, this is only a protection mechanism for product innovations, and even there it may not be efficient.

Protection is thus a problem. In the current period of rapid economic change and innovation, it often avails little to protect innovations by formal means (except patents for some product innovations). The best protection for the firm is constant innovation, and staying in front of the competition. This will both ensure a series of innovations and create an image as an innovative firm.

15.   Innovation and Organizational Learning

The next part of the discussion of the strategic innovation theory concerns how the experience of innovation processes is accumulated and used to improve future innovation processes. It may be assumed that firms will attempt to do this.

Organizational learning impinges on two aspects of innovation: it makes the firm a better innovator and it brings about many small changes. As stated in Chapter 3, some changes are not reproduced. It was also stated in that chapter (Section 4.3) that firms will attempt to reproduce the small unreproduced changes through organizational learning. I will now return to these changes.

Concerning the issue of firms becoming better innovators, we now come to a level above that of innovation activities – to a learning loop which comes after the concrete innovation processes. The learning loop is an organizational process, but is based on individual learning, as will be argued in this chapter. This means that many parties and individuals in the organization participate in the learning process, but the manager has a special role. He or she has responsibility for ensuring that learning takes place (and has responsibility if learning does not take place). This responsibility is expressed by the different roles that the manager can have in the learning process. These roles will be discussed in this chapter.

Organizational learning is not a new subject; it has been quite popular for the last decade (cf. the popularity of books by Argyris 1992; Nonaka and Takeuchi 1995), even in innovation theory (Lundvall 1988). Here I will discuss it within the framework of the strategic innovation theory, which will provide another perspective and will complete the account of the theory.

1 WHAT IS ORGANIZATIONAL LEARNING?

1.1 The Rational and Processual View

Organizational learning has been defined in many ways; and interpretations of the concept are complex and varied. Basically, there are two extremes. At one extreme, organizational learning is interpreted as knowledge (for example,

Nonaka and Takeuchi 1995, Machlup 1983); this knowledge may be explicit or tacit (cf. Polanyi 1966), but in principle it can be explicit if we find the right methods for making tacit knowledge explicit. In principle one can complete the knowledge-acquiring process when one makes all the knowledge explicit and codifies it so that all members of the organization have access to it. This interpretation is in accordance with the traditional, rational view of economics.

The other extreme sees organizational learning as a never-ending social process (for example, Argyris and Schön 1978; Senge 1995). Learning is about behaviour – how we do things (cf. Argyris and Schön's (1978) theory-in-use). It is a complex pattern of knowledge, behavioural habits, and experience, norms and values. In the perfect learning organization every member would have this pattern internalized as part of their 'me' (cf. Mead 1934). This takes a long time, and it must be done for every new member who enters the organization. Since it is done in interaction with other people, mutual influences arise which can very easily turn the learning in a new direction. This is not only because new knowledge can appear during the interaction process; it is also because prestige and other social status factors influence the process. Thus before the new members, and perhaps the old ones too, have internalized the learning (how to do things) in their 'me', new learning has already arisen in the system. That is why Argyris and Schön (1978) state that organizational learning is an ideal that can never be achieved in reality; although firms can strive for it. this is expressed in Figure 15.1.

Figure 15.1   Views of organizational learning

Knowledge   Behaviour

Rational   ⟵————————————————⟶   Process

Here we will deal with learning in a specific sense, namely learning about innovation processes. Thus this chapter is not about learning in general. The interpretation that I will use here is mostly at the right end of the scale: organizational learning as a social process. This is in accordance with the interpretation of the innovation process that I have developed in earlier chapters. However, learning in relation to innovation can also be a more rational process in which explicit knowledge is most important and tacit knowledge, at least in principle, can be explicit and codified. This is the situation in most R&D activities and accords with the scientific way of thinking. Since most innovation theory (at least within the technological–economic paradigm (cf. Sundbo 1998b) sees innovation as completely or primarily identical to R&D, it is no wonder that the rational, knowledge-based interpretation of learning (left end of the scale) has become the norm in innovation theory (cf. for example the annual surveys drawn up by Eurostat). This will also form part of the interpretation here, because R&D is part of the innovative organization, as stated in the foregoing chapters. However, the processual view, which has the same logic as the dual organization model, is considered to provide the major explanation within the strategic framework.

1.2   The Elements of Innovative Learning

This brings us to an understanding of the elements of innovative learning. It consists of three elements:

Knowledge	Knowledge consists of experience-based and theoretically internalized facts. It may be knowledge about how to do something or not to do something, or just facts that we can do nothing about except store them. Learning is about storing new facts, and developing a system of deciding which facts to store and which to retrieve in certain situations.

Knowledge may be: *explicit*: Codified so everyone can have access to it; or

                            tacit: Internalized in individuals who have not codified it for other people.

Action	Action is the ability to do things. This is an individual factor, but much of it can be learned by other people. It is not fact-based, but is a physical or intellectual capability. It is often hidden, but can be explained to other people, who may – or may not – be able to copy it. Learning is about experience of which acts are efficient in certain situations.

It may be: *individual*: The individual performs the act himself; or

          interactional: The act is performed by two or more people.

Creativity   Creativity is the ability to invent new knowledge (and question existing knowledge) and new ways of solving problems or creating a better situation. This comes from the hidden personality of individuals. Learning is about the individual gaining experience and realizing how he or she could be more creative. The creativity of one individual cannot be copied by another, but situations that improve the creativity of all individuals can be created.

It may be: *individual*:   The creativity of individuals; or
            team-based: The creativity that can arise from interaction process in teams.

Organizational learning is the combination of knowledge, action and creativity. As before, we can talk about these as resources or 'stocks' which exist within the individuals in the organization. These resources are thus individual. Put differently, organizational learning capability can be formulated as the organization's ability to make these resources common to all the relevant members of the organization. In practice the management will be responsible for this, that is, the managerial structure as it has been defined in the earlier chapters.

One can also talk about competencies rather than learning: the stock of knowledge, action-resources and creativity among individuals that makes up their competencies, while the firm's competence is its ability (that is, the managerial structure's ability) to get the individuals to store such resources and to share the 'stock'.

The model of Argyris and Schön (1978) is highly relevant here. It operates with three loops in organizational learning. Single-loop learning consists of experience that leads directly to innovations (employees learn about customer needs or new technical possibilities). Double-loop learning changes the preparedness to learn; norms and behaviour become learning-oriented. Deutero-learning is learning about how one learns (for example, how to organize the learning process).

This is the interpretation of organizational learning about innovation activities that will form the basis of this chapter.

2 WHY DO FIRMS CREATE A LEARNING ORGANIZATION IN ORDER TO INNOVATE AND CHANGE?

This is about two things:

1. How firms seek to manage the unreproduced, unsystematic small changes. This cannot be done by codifying all learning and making it explicit because these changes are so varied and develop in different situations. Often they are the results of highly individual learning. The interactive learning process (the right end of the scale in Figure 15.1) is the relevant type of learning here, and the manager must ensure that it is taking place.
2. How firms seek to make the systematic innovation process more efficient. This may still require interactive learning process, but it also calls for codified, explicit learning (the left side of the scale in Figure 15.1). It often consists of R&D activities, which are based on scientific knowledge that can be codified. Even when it consists of project-organized innovation activities, firms must try to codify learning about how to organize such activities. The knowledge element is stronger in this situation than is the case with the unreproduced changes.

Organizational learning, and thus the task that managers have to deal with, has a dual function: on the one hand to promote high levels of creativity, problem-solving activity and knowledge procurement; and on the other hand to restrict this so that not all the resources are devoted to learning about how to make innovations (some must be spent on actually making them, and on the daily production activities). The principle of balance that was introduced with relation to the management of innovation also applies to learning about innovation activities. This also takes us a step further up: management can learn to be better at maintaining this balance.

The search for a learning organization, in relation to innovation activities as well as other things, expresses the managers' goal of creating a rational organization which they can oversee and control. If we cannot create innovations when we actually want them and if we cannot control the innovation process, let us see if we can develop a system for doing this by learning from the past and systematizing such learning; such a system will help us in the future.

Organizational learning about innovation involves a struggle between the rational goal of a codified systematization of knowledge, and the creation of a culture that permits individuals in the organization to learn for themselves without management needing to constantly guide the process. It can be assumed that managers will try to force the process towards the rational goal, but in many situations they will try to develop a self-generating learning organization by simply ensuring that there is a learning culture. The striving for the rational goal will never succeed, among other reasons because the market and the environment in general change and the firm will be forced to develop a new strategy. This will make much of the former knowledge invalid and irrelevant. That is why the recent attempt to measure innovation and learning capacity by measuring knowledge and formal R&D activities (by Eurostat) reveals only part of the innovation activities and learning capacity of firms. It does not measure the interactive, processual aspects of learning.

Thus the processual learning system will be the dominant one. However, this system can be overruled in some situations by a systematic, science-based innovation process of the type we know from R&D departments, and we can learn to perfect the management of these processes. The attempt to put human beings on the moon follows this path. However, it is part of the basic assumption in this book that such rational paths are becoming increasingly rare in business firms, at least outside the high-tech industry, and perhaps even within it.

Another event that can overrule the system is the appearance of a classic entrepreneur: one who does not learn anything but just acts and succeeds. Classic entrepreneurship, where a single person creates a radical innovation and a new firm, cannot be learned. Entrepreneurship is a personality factor that has developed during upbringing (cf. McClelland 1961). However, this situation too is becoming increasingly rare – cf. Schumpeter's conclusion as early as 1943 (Schumpeter 1943).

3 THE EVOLUTIONARY ASPECT OF ORGANIZATIONAL LEARNING ABOUT INNOVATION

Organizational learning is an aspect of the evolutionary system in which firms participate. A firm participates in the evolutionary process, which means that it attempts to survive and grow in a competitive market. This is done by innovating. However, the firm's fight for survival and growth has some extra layers besides the immediate innovation activity. The firm attempts consciously to consider its innovative survival behaviour and to steer it. This has two layers. The first is the attempt to guide the process by setting up a strategy which expresses where the firm wants to go and how it can get there. The evolutionary aspect is the struggle with competitors in the market where one deploys one's own strengths and exploits competitors' weaknesses to win, and this is included in the strategy. But however good a strategy one formulates, developments are rarely as successful and free of backlash as one might wish. The firm therefore attempts to learn from its mistakes so it can do better next time. This is the layer of organizational learning.

We thus have three levels of economic evolution shown in Figure 15.2.

Figure 15.2   *The evolutionary process of the firm*

Level	Process	Result
First level	Fight for survival and possible growth (development of the firm):	INNOVATION
Second level	Attempt to control the development process:	STRATEGY
Third level	Attempt to improve the development process and its control	ORGANIZATIO-NAL LEARNING

This is a modification of Argyris and Schön's three-loop model. The second level here emphasizes strategy, where Argyris and Schön emphasized norms, behavioural patterns and so on. This is because the strategic innovation theory leans slightly more to the rational side than Argyris and Schön's model.

The activities at all three levels are social activities that take place within the organization. The members of the organization engage in actions and interactions. This is a trial-and-error process, but it is not a planless trial from scratch every time. The members of the organization try to learn to do things better. This learning is at first individual, but may at the next stage be shared by all members of the organization. This is not an easy process, as discussed above: learning is difficult to share because it is difficult to codify. Information and communication technology may be used to share the learning, but this is only an instrument of communication and does not create learning by itself.

Management plays a particular role in this evolutionary process as 'coach', a word that been used in popular organizational literature to characterize the manager's new role: he is not the person who decides everything by issuing orders but the person who ensures that evolution takes place. He inspires the employees and regulates their behaviour.

The process of evolution is not a planned process, but it is not completely anarchic or chaotic. It is a regulated social process. In their evolutionary theory, Nelson and Winter (1982) described the evolution mechanism in terms of routines. They consider strategy to be management's heuristic attempts to find and institutionalize new and better routines, including innovation routines. In the framework established in this analysis, I do not see evolutionary activities as institutionalized (taking on a fixed routine form) as Nelson and Winter do by emphasizing routines. I see them as more organic: they are often different in form and content (although many elements are repeated). Learning is not expressed in activity and interaction routines. It is a pattern of knowledge, actions and creativity that forms a common background for all the members of the organization, but specific actions are not fixed. The evolutionary mechanisms at all three levels are flexible, and are influenced by creativity-based changes and interaction sequences that vary from situation to situation.

The routine model that Nelson and Winter set up is valid for a certain group of firms, those that are highly R&D-based. They will very often have routinized their innovation-making and organizational learning processes, which is easy for them because they can base this on scientific traditions and methods. This is the type of firm that Nelson and Winter are thinking of in the formulation of their evolutionary theory (which can primarily be placed within the technology–economic paradigm of innovation theories). However, in firms based on the broad strategic innovation process described in this book, it is not the best course to assume that the 'genes' of innovation and learning processes are routines, as Nelson and Winter say. It is a little ambitious to talk about genes in social sciences, even when they are used as a metaphor. If we were to talk about genes – or fundamental elements of the evolution of the firm – within the framework of the strategic innovation theory, they would be of several kinds and would include the following (compared with the three evolutionary levels stated above):

- interaction and action patterns (including organizational culture)
- the management's interpretation of the environment (including the markets); and
- the management's 'coaching' pattern.

I have already used the metaphor of 'soft' evolutionary theory (ecology) from biology; this is logical, because it expresses the idea of a complex and flexible system where one cannot predict who will survive.

4 ORGANIZATION OF ORGANIZATIONAL LEARNING

The kinds of competencies that are needed in learning about innovation are twofold (cf. Argyris and Schön 1978):

1. Intellectual competence, which is the learning stock and the ability to mobilize earlier learning that is stored in the mind of individuals. This competence exists permanently in individuals.
2. Interpersonal competence, which is the ability of individuals to cooperate in innovative interaction processes. This kind of competence only exists in situations where people interact in an innovation process. There are many elements in interaction processes; they shift from situation to situation and the course of interaction is different every time, even if the same individuals are involved. The competence needed is therefore different each time, and this makes learning difficult.

This is because organizational learning is not a formalized, codified system (as, for example, Nelson and Winter's routines are). It is a social system where the players change their norms and behaviour. Organizations are not considered as fixed, bureaucratic or Fordist units, but as flexible, continuously changing ones (cf. Volberda 1998; Wood 1988). Learning is a combination of cognitive knowledge (intellectual competence), creativity and interactional skills (interpersonal competence) and requires an interaction system. This cannot simply be created from above if it is to be innovative; the social system itself must be prepared to learn, to store the learning and to use it in new, creative ways. On the other hand, the learning must be controlled to ensure that it is shared (that is, becomes organizational).

Here again dual organization is the model that can be used to describe what happens in organizational learning. The cognitive process of acquiring knowledge takes place within the individual employee and interaction skills are developed in the loosely coupled interaction structure, where they are stored as norms and shared patterns of action and interaction. Those norms and patterns are mostly tacit, but they can be made explicit, at least to some degree. They are often shared by only a part of the organization, and even if they are made explicit or codified, they may be difficult for others to understand and imitate. The groups in the organization have no natural incentive to share these patterns of learning with other parts of the organization. Only if a particular group interacts with another group, and the learning is important to the first group in this situation, does this group have some incentive to share the learning with the other group.

The managerial structure therefore needs to create a system that can make knowledge common to all members of the organization, or at least to all relevant members. There has been some discussion of knowledge-sharing as part of organizational learning (that is, one individual informs others of his knowledge). This is an aspect that management must ensure, but it must also ensure that learning about interaction skills (interpersonal competencies) is shared.

This is not easy. First we have all the problems of identifying and codifying learning and sharing it. But in addition learning is an instrument of power and conflicts can arise over learning. Some groups or individuals may attempt to keep their learning to themselves, because that will give them a better position of power in the firm or in the labour market in general. I found an example of this in financial service companies, where the information technology department exhibited behaviour that brought it into conflict with other departments. These problems are the reason why no managers in the cases that I studied would say that they had a learning organization. Information and communication technology is a core instrument in knowledge-sharing, but it does not prevent conflicts and selfishness.

Opinions can differ as to which type of learning is the most important and what means should be used to make people share it. Management thus also has to intervene in these socio-political processes to ensure shared organizational learning. This process often happens harmoniously between the managerial structure and the loosely coupled interactive structure, but sometimes there is conflict between them. There may also be conflict between different groups within the loosely coupled interactive structure.

Management needs to establish a policy for organizational learning, because otherwise it will have difficulty controlling the process. This policy can be included in the strategy. However, the strategy will only express the firm's overall goals, typically the fact that it wants to have a learning organization. The means to be used to learn and to make this learning common to the whole organization must be developed in an operational scheme that is used and corrected as part of the daily management work.

However, the organization of the innovation learning process can in practice have different degrees of intentionality and management (or institutionalization). A model of these different forms is given in Figure 15.3 (cf. Sundbo 1998a).

Figure 15.3   Different forms of organization of innovation learning processes

MANAGEMENT DIMENSION

← Systema- →►◄— Open →
   tised

			Strategy	Managed	Collective	Intrapre-neur
INTEN-TIONAL	Pro-active	Search-learn	1	3	6	9
	Pro-active	Active cognition	2	4	7	10
DIMEN-SION	Reactive	Ex-post learning	-	5	8	-
	Passive	Non-learning	11	-	-	-

This diagram is based on case studies of a catering company, an insurance company and a consultancy firm. Specific enterprises can be placed in different cells of the figure, which is bidimensional.

The first dimension is intentionality. What are the intentions of the company with respect to organizational learning processes? Does the company consciously organize the learning process – or certain individuals (intrapreneurs) within the company? This dimension characterizes the intention of the company – how active the learning system is, whether it is conscious and intentional, or random and driven by circumstances.

The intentional dimension ranges from the most active, high-risk, intentional learning process to a non-learning situation. At one end of this dimension is the search-learn category. Companies in this category try to launch isolated, often fairly radical, innovations, the success of which cannot be anticipated or predicted in any detail. The next category, active cognition, is a more highly planned, proactive learning process. The companies try to create coherence in the development and learning process. Innovation processes take place, but they are not as experimental as in the search-learn situation. The third category is the reactive learning process. The company's learning process is based on ex-post learning (adaptive learning). This means that the company learns from its experiences (typically the negative ones). These experiences, however, remain experiences, in the sense that they are not immediately systematized and applied in an attempt to generate better knowledge and more preparedness for future action. The experience is put aside until a similar situation happens to arise, or until the company later formulates a strategy or makes other important decisions. At the other extreme of this dimension is the non-learning situation, where the organization does not accumulate any experience and learns nothing. This is an entirely passive process.

The other dimension shown in Figure 15.3 is the managerial dimension; that is, how the learning process progresses and is managed within the framework of the existing intentional system. This comes after the intention stage – when the event that could be learned from has happened. Is there a conscious attempt to store the experience gained as learning? Who ensures that there is a beneficial learning process? Is it an open process where nobody is held responsible, or is the process managed with some elements that ensure institutionalization of the learning process? This depends on the degree of management versus anarchy.

The managerial dimension is a scale with strategy at the most 'managed' end. Companies in this category have a plan or a strategy that has been designed or confirmed by management, which also controls the learning process. The next category is the managed learning process. In this category an overall plan or strategy is absent or weak, but management still takes responsibility for actively ensuring the gathering and accumulation of knowledge and experience. In both these categories the learning process is systematized in one way or another. By this I mean that to some degree the management takes care of the learning process. In the third category, the collective learning process, the management is not the entity which ensures the learning process. This is done broadly by the entire organization, or by a number of members of the organization. It takes an open (non-systematized) form (in the loosely coupled interactive structure). It may be collective or individual, depending on whether routines for gathering knowledge and experience are developed. The last category is the intrapreneurial form, where the knowledge is possessed by individual members of the organization, that is, the intrapreneurs. The intrapreneurship process must be an open one, since it involves a high degree of creativity and a certain element of anarchy.

In the figure, numbering indicates the different variants of the learning organization. Not all of the combinations in the model can be assumed to exist or to be logically possible.

Some learning will be common to all members of the organization. This is general learning. Some learning will only be common to a certain group of professionals or experts. This is expert knowledge related to the special field of a defined group of experts. This applies not only to their cognitive knowledge, but also to their interactional skills, which may be confined to the particular expert group.

5 INSTRUMENTS FOR MAKING THE LEARNING COLLECTIVE

If learning and knowledge are to be shared, methods and instruments must be developed to make this happen. Various methods and instruments exist that the management can use, and others will be invented in the future. None of these are miraculous cures that can guarantee organizational learning, which must still be considered a never-obtainable ideal. Examples of methods and instruments that I have found in my empirical research are mentioned below.

There are two parts of the learning process, as mentioned before: one is the storing of the experience, the other is its mobilization when necessary.

5.1 Making Experience Shared

The first problem is to store experience so that the stock is common to all – or all the relevant – people in the organization. The experience can be explicit or tacit (like knowledge – however, experience in this sense is more than knowledge, it is also the ability to act and to be creative). Thus one method is to make it explicit, while another is to know where the tacit experience is located (which individuals, departments, teams have the experience). This can be – and has been – done in small firms (examples from my case studies are a bank, a medium-sized cleaning company and a consultancy firm with 10 to 15 employees).

In Fígure 15.4 I mention examples of methods and instruments that the manager can use to ensure that the experience is generally accessible or that people know who has the experience.

Figure 15.4 Methods for making learning organizational

Codification (making the experience explicit)	Tacit experience (knowing where to find it)
Writing manuals (describing 'how to') *(example: an instrument manufacturing company)* Storing the experience in a shared information technology database *(examples: a bank, a management consultancy firm)* Creating a catalogue of experts and knowledge *(example: an engineering consultancy firm)*	One person becomes the bearer of the experience (the 'foreman' or leader) *(example: a company producing printing plates)* A knowledge-collecting group ('the expert group') *(example: a bank)* Overlapping group structure (individuals from one project team participate in the next one) *(example: a firm of consultant engineers)* Collective memory (experience becomes part of the corporate culture) *(examples: a firm of engineering consultants, a management consultancy firm)*

The process of making tacit knowledge explicit or at least making it sharable, is difficult. Nonaka and Takeuchi (1995) have launched a model of how such a process could be developed. It starts with the sharing of tacit knowledge through informal social processes. Afterwards the shared knowledge becomes increasingly explicit and systematized through the creation of concepts and systematic development projects (prototypes). Senge (1995) has also drawn up a model of organizational development which has five phases, from the individual vision of development and learning to the stage where learning becomes part of a common system.

5.2   How to Mobilize the Experience

The second problem is when and how to mobilize the experience – that is, the learning capability. This is a management problem and one of the most difficult competencies to develop. This is generally the point at which the process of developing a learning organization stops (as the example in the next section will demonstrate). The learning capability is placed at the third level of the evolutionary process (see Figure 15.2): the experience of how and when the firm has most efficiently mobilized its learning experience in the past, plus a creativity factor because a new situation often develops to which the learning of the past must be adapted.

Argyris (1992) emphasizes the many barriers to developing an efficient learning capability. He warns against using over-formal methods, because a good deal of psychological behaviour and creativity is involved in this, and formal methods and planning cannot ensure that a manager mobilizes the experience at the right time and in the right way. Senge (1995) talks about establishing an early warning system – by giving attention to small symptoms indicating that innovation activities are not taking the course suitable to the actual situation of the firm. The managers thus have to define the types of symptoms to observe, which again is difficult, because these differ from firm to firm and from situation to situation. Nonaka and Takeuchi (1995) emphasize knowledge in particular and talk about a system where many parts of the firm participate in mobilizing knowledge. They take a broad view of the managerial structure and stress the role of middle managers in particular. The middle managers are closer to daily practice and are therefore more sensitive to problems and possibilities. They observe the symptoms first and they know the experience resources best.

The general issues are whether the learning capability (experience-mobilizing) system should be formalized or intuitive, and whether the top manager should control the system or this should be left to the broader managerial structure which includes middle managers. These issues are summarized in Figure 15.5.

Figure 15.5 Model of learning capacity

| | | *Leadership of the learning capability* | |
		Top manager	Broad management structure
The process is	Formalized	a	b
	Intuitive	c	d

There are four possibilities. The formalized top management variant (a) means that top managers store the experience formally, for example in plans, in systematic methods for evaluating the firm's situation on the market and, perhaps, using theories that they have learned. The formalized broad managerial structure variant (b) means that certain procedures and routines have been set up in the organization so that the issue of whether to change the learning system is raised regularly. The intuitive top management variant (c) means that the top manager decides when to mobilize the learning experience, but he does so intuitively – when he feels it is necessary. If he is a charismatic type af leader, he is able to make the organization mobilize the learning experience at the right time. The last variant, intuitive broad management (d), is the anarchic situation where there is no leadership of the mobilizing process, but a number of people in various parts of the organization intuitively initiate experience mobilization.

There may be a conflictual relationship between the managerial structure and the experts (or professional groups) or individuals in the loosely coupled interactive structure. The loyalties and learning frame of reference of the professionals or experts are divided between two parties, the firm and the profession (or similar experts in other firms). Often they choose the profession because this is most likely to guarantee their future in the labour market. They also often come into conflict with management, because professionals want to make learning elitist, that is, keep it to themselves and store and use it in accordance with professional norms. Managers are interested in making the learning common to everyone in the firm or in keeping control of it themselves. They do not have full control over learning that is stored and used according to professional norms (I saw this in all cases related to information technology personnel and in some insurance companies in relation to other professionals such as actuaries). This potential conflict does not arise in professional firms (such as architectural, consultancy or accountancy firms) because the managers in such firms also operate within the professional paradigm.

6   CONDITIONS FOR AND BARRIERS TO THE DEVELOPMENT OF A LEARNING ORGANIZATION

The learning innovation organization is a difficult thing to realize. Specific conditions must be fulfilled if it is to be developed, and there are many possible obstacles. These will be discussed in this section using a case study.[2] This will make it easier to demonstrate the conditions.

The theoretical framework for this case analysis is 'extended barter'. This theory was developed by myself and some colleagues on the basis of studies in manufacturing and service firms in Denmark (Bevort, Pedersen and Sundbo 1992; Bevort, Sundbo, Pedersen 1995). However, the same phenomenon has also been observed in other countries such as the UK (Storey 1992). The theory says that in many present-day firms the demands on the employees are more extensive than in typical Fordist firms (cf. Lipietz 1987). They must be flexible in place, time and function; they must involve themselves in the firm's activities, including its innovation activities; they must retrain continuously, and they must themselves assume responsibility for this. Employees must to a great extent be self-managing, middle managers functioning as supporters and as personnel managers. Meanwhile the management of the work task is often up to the employee himself. Employees for their part are also making new demands on their working life, as Danish investigations demonstrate (Bevort, Sundbo and Pedersen 1995). They want an interesting job where they are challenged to develop their skills and competencies, and they may also want social and welfare goods (such as sports facilities) from the firm, a social life at the workplace and so on.

All these extended demands and expectations from both sides are together termed 'extended barter'. The firm and the employees not only exchange a certain amount of standard work for a certain amount of money as in the Fordist period, but want a number of other benefits. What each party wants from the other party and what the other wants to give in return can vary. The barter process is therefore not so much an issue of reaching general agreements between unions and employer associations, but of continuous negotiation. This negotiation process is more decentralized than the Fordist bargaining process, and often takes place between individual employees and middle managers.

---

[2] This section was included in an article in *Employee Relations* (Sundbo 1999). It is published here by agreement with MCB University Press.

The case in question concerns the empowerment of employees and middle managers in the innovation process. It emphasizes the interaction between the managerial structure and the loosely coupled interactive structure, and thus illustrates how the dual innovation organization can work successfully.

6.1 The Case Study

The case studied was a small Danish retail bank (Lån & Spar Bank, here called L&S), with 275 employees and its main activities in Copenhagen. Its strategy was market segmentation, and it targeted middle-income private customers. It was studied in the period 1996 to 1999.

The bank did not see much development until the present general manager was engaged in 1988. He is an entrepreneur type who has changed L&S into an innovative, fast-growing enterprise.

L&S traditionally has an active, motivating personnel policy which delegates responsibility to employees and attempts to involve them in the firm. There are many young employees; the average age is 35 and the average term of employment is seven years.

6.2 Creating a Learning Organization: Description of the Empowerment Programme in L&S

In its strategic analyses L&S reached certain conclusions.

Technology – which here means information and communication technology – was seen as a possible innovative resource. L&S had been very active in introducing new technology and using it for product innovations. They were the first bank in Denmark to introduce 'second-generation' home banking in the 1990s (the first generation was introduced in the 1980s – cf. Sundbo 1991a). The problem was that when the large banks decided to develop home banking and other product-oriented technologies, they had much greater resources and thus a possible competitive advantage.

The bank wanted to build on human resources as the future core development factor. It had no particular financial strength and – as a small bank – did not have a very strong quantitative market position (a large market share). It did have a strong qualitative market position: it was very well known because it was innovative and offered the best prices to private customers, and had grown more than any other Danish bank for a period. It had a good resource in its strong customer loyalty. However, this was a somewhat unreliable factor since bank customers were tending to shop around more for the lowest prices (Sundbo 1997). Even with this factor, the behaviour of employees was the crucial element. This led the management to adopt the strategy that the human factor was the only thing the bank could rely on in its future development.

The bank created an organizational development programme based on the idea of the learning organization and strategy development. Several projects were created under the programme. Its goal was for employees to improve their professional and customer-handling competencies. They were to participate in strategy formulation and the innovation process. The bank was to learn in general from the projects so that it could improve its ability to develop the organization and make innovations in the future.

The *first* project of the learning organization involved managers at all levels. They were supposed to learn to work in teams. The programme also attempted to explain to them what a learning organization is.

The managers were supposed to spread this knowledge. They were to go back to their employees, involve them in the development of the learning organization and explain to them what a learning organization is. No special resources were allocated for this, neither time nor money. Middle managers and employees were supposed to develop a learning organization as part of their normal work alongside their other tasks.

The *second* project was a group-oriented innovation project. It was a phased model which involved the employees (cf. Sundbo 1997), who could send proposals for innovations to the management. These could be new product ideas or other ideas, for example for organizational or process changes. If the management found the idea interesting, the employee – or employees – could establish a development group to develop the idea further. The group was to be self-managing. After a phase of idea development, management decided whether the idea should be developed into a product, an organizational change or whatever the object was. If it was decided to continue, the last phase of development took place in a new group, a task force which had expertise in the specific field.

The *third* project had a more general aim. Its aim was to involve employees and managers in the strategy process (this was the main aim), as well asin innovation activities and to improve their behaviour in daily work, for example the treatment of customers, teamwork, the use of technology. The project was organized as a series of workshops with exercises. Some of the exercises were continued after the workshops. The participants were supposed to work in groups on an everyday basis as well as carrying out their normal activities.

The *fourth* project was a personal development programme. It had the aim of developing the competencies of employees to the advantage of the bank as well as the employee, who was given general competencies that could be useful in other jobs. All courses included practical group work. One of these was a ten-hour exercise to develop a new bank product as part of a team. This exercise could lead to ideas that would be implemented as innovations in L&S.

6.3 The Dual Organization and the Learning Loops

The goal of the programme as stated by the top manager of L&S was to create a self-generating learning organization. This means an organization that automatically learns at all three levels described in the model drawn up by Argyris and Schön (1978), in other words, an innovation and learning process which takes place entirely within the loosely coupled interactive structure. However, in practice this proved only partially to be the case. What happened was a dual organizational process with a dialectic between the top-down process in the managerial structure and the bottom-up process in the loosely coupled interactive structure.

The development of the learning organization in L&S is progressing through the three stages that Argyris and Schön introduced, but in a different order to the one they specify.

The first phase in the L&S programme was planned double-loop learning: it was intended to make employees and managers innovation and learning-oriented. This was a phase of empowerment and motivation where the management attempted to create an innovative and learning-oriented culture in the bank (cf. Hodgson's (1998) statement that competence is part of the corporate culture).

When the employees and managers have become innovation- and learning-oriented, they are supposed to formulate innovation ideas and projects themselves, and in this process learn which innovations are best and how the innovation process can best be organized. This is single-loop learning, which is the second phase.

The management of the bank hopes that later, in a third phase, deutero-learning will be developed, that is, the the bank will become a self-learning organization. Double-loop learning projects can always be initiated by the management, but they cost a great deal in resources. Thus it is best if the organization – meaning the employees themselves – changes the organizational learning system in the future without new, comprehensive empowerment training programmes having to be established.

On the basis of their experience in the first two phases, the employees and management are supposed to develop a decentralized organization for learning to learn.

6.4 What are the Conditions for Success?

This case study can form the basis for a theoretical model of the conditions for the interplay between the two structures of the dual innovation organization. This model is based on the idea of extended barter between employees and the firm.

The model operates on three levels, following Argyris and Schön's (1978) theory. Both management and employees must give and take at all levels.

Level 1: Creation of a learning culture

The first level is double-loop learning. It can be compared, in a planned development process as in the L&S, to the first phase of motivation – competence-building and involvement. It has been a success. Many employees and middle managers have been empowered and are involved in the bank's development problems. Only a minority seem to have developed real corporate entrepreneurial competencies, but the fact that some have done so means that one can assess the programme as a success in terms of the goals for innovation activities.

At the phase related to the expected goals for innovation, things become less precise. Both parties will gain certain benefits here, and they may be satisfied with that, which means that the organization will not establish the next level (or go on to the next phase in the planned development process).

The firm	*The employees*
will gain the general involvement of employees (including middle managers).	will gain personal skills that may be useful to them in their future careers (ability to involve themselves, cooperate and so on) as well as a more varied and interesting job.

If successful, this will produce general motivation for corporate entrepreneurship, and for other developments such as a more flexible organization and willingness and ability to learn.

For this level to be realized one of the following two conditions must be fulfilled:

1. *The management must establish major programmes for developing the organization and the employees' competencies and entrepreneurial orientation.* All parts of the organization must be involved – all employees and all levels of managers. This requires many resources, but if they are not invested the process will not be sufficient to create the necessary competencies and entrepreneurial action orientation.

2. *An innovation and entrepreneurial-oriented culture must already exist.* This might for example be the case if the enterprise is located in a region with an entrepreneurial culture.

Level 2: Development of innovative behaviour

The first level is not sufficient to create innovations, which require active intrapreneurship and single-loop learning. The firm may be content to stay at level 1 and gain a more motivated and generally well-qualified workforce, but sometimes it wants more – that is toi say innovations. This phase has also been successful at L&S, although slightly less so thanphase 1. The development process has been extremely fast and the project teams and the interplay between them and the management have worked. Innovative ideas have been produced, but they were not as many or as important as the management had hoped.

The benefits for the parties at this level are as follows.

The firm	*The employees*
will gain active corporate entrepreneurship and innovations.	will receive specific, traditionally prestigious rewards in the form of promotion, money, more independence in their work and so on.

The problem is how the firm can get from level 1 to level 2. For this, the following conditions must be fulfilled:

1. *The employees must have intrapreneurial skills.* The urge to be an intrapreneur must be developed, and the potential intrapreneurs must learn some practical skills such as efficient teamwork. There has been some discussion of whether entrepreneurship can be learned or is a personality one has from one's childhood (for example, Sexton and Kasarda 1992). The assumption here (cf. also Drucker 1985, Sundbo 1992), which is supported by the L&S case, is that intrapreneurship is a role that can be learned – at least to a certain extent.
2. *The management must react fast and select the ideas to be developed further,* and must support intrapreneurial activities.
3. *The extended barter situation must be set up.* The rewards must be more specific than at the first level. One cannot give general rules for this; it is a game that requires different methods in different situations. Perhaps the management can persuade the employees that level 1 rewards are satisfactory, or the employees themselves will come to that conclusion. If not, the management will have to bargain with the employees about how to get to level 2 rewards and what exactly these should be. Such a barter situation could be formal and general (for example, a certain reward for those who propose good ideas), but it will probably be more efficient if it is informal and individual.

Level 3: The self-generating learning organization

The final problem is deutero-learning. Will the organization develop a self-generating learning organization? If not, empowerment projects (or other change projects) must be implemented constantly, and this means permanently high costs.

Where the competencies – except those from the collective corporate culture aspect of th motivation at level 1 – are mostly individual at levels 1 and 2, they must be organizational at level 3.

Organizational learning will have two levels. One is the formal level where each department creates knowledge and routines as official procedures, for example at annual seminars where problems and solutions are debated. The other level involves the treatment of tacit knowledge. This means informal procedures for storing and perhaps culturally codifying experience and knowledge (that is, putting them into words that are recognized by the employees as part of the company language). This is part of the corporate culture, which thus must be developed.

Organizational learning can also be organized in a flexible way – something in between the formalized and the tacit way. This is, for example, the case with the knowledge centres at L&S. Networked information and communication technology databases are the basis for exchanging knowledge, and the experience is stored in these databases as a form of learning. A similar system has been used in management consultancy firms.

This level is the most difficult to achieve, as shown by the case of L&S, which has not wholly reached this level. It is difficult for employees to participate in the organization and collecting of knowledge of how to learn, because it is something different from the daily work most of them do, and does not give them the same prestige as specific innovations which is related to the production field.

What the firm gains at this level is obvious: a learning organization that requires a minimum of management resources. It is more difficult to see what the employees get out of it. They do get the competence represented by having participated in such a process, which could be a qualification if they later move to another firm. However, this is a very general competence that is difficult to document, so it will probably be of limited value to the employees.

The benefits of the extended barter situation can be summarized as follows.

The firm	*The employees*
will gain a self-generating learning organization, which saves management resources.	will gain general experience of working in a learning organization.

It is impossible or at least very difficult to develop an individual reward system that would satisfy employees as directly as at levels 1 and 2. The extended bartering has to be structural here. This means that there will be no particular reward; participation at level 3 will be a natural part of the normal work. And this is indeed how it was widely considered, for example in the insurance companies I studied. If employees have relatively free conditions for developing their own work and there is pressure from the management to do this, learning will become part of their normal work. The benefit they gain from participating in level 3 is that they can do their work better, and thus they can keep their jobs.

Thus it is difficult to reach level 3. The first, plus one or more of the rest, of the following conditions must be fulfilled to reach this level.

1. There must be pressure on the employees to develop their work, and a certain freedom for them to do so.
2. The deutero-learning must be organized. Either routines that store the experience must be developed in the organization, or the deutero-learning must be institutionalized in one department, for example, a Human Resource Management department.
3. A corporate culture that emphasizes the existence of a learning organization must be developed. The culture must be aware of all the changes inside and outside the firm, and of the fact that these changes require new organizational learning. The culture must be very flexible and change-oriented.
4. There must be a flexible formal learning system based, for example, on networked information and communication technology databases. Such a system combines the free exchange of knowledge and solutions to problems with the formally structured storage of knowledge in the databases.

PART IV

The Macro Level

16.   Economic Development in Society: The Interaction Economy

So far the strategic innovation theory has been discussed at the micro level – the level of the firm. In this chapter I will discuss it at the macro level: how can economic development in society be understood within the framework of this theory?

The strategic innovation theory makes a proposal which will be developed into a model in the next chapter. This chapter will discuss the issue of how economic development in society is determined. The general approach of this book has been to explain this in terms of sociological factors, and this will also be the case in this part. Since interaction has been a core concept in explaining innovation at the micro level, this will also be the case at the macro level. The economic model for explaining development is thus called the interaction economy.

1   A MACRO MODEL AND ITS BASIS

The aim of the last two chapters was to use the discussion in previous chapters to develop a model of economic development. In them I discussed innovation at the micro (that is, firm) level. This is relevant to the understanding of the behaviour of the firm and may be of practical relevance to managers.

It may, however, be of interest to develop the discussion and take it to the macro level. There is a theoretical and a practical interest in investigating the issue of how an industry or a nation develops economically. The practical interest relates to the political ideal of developing industries so that the national or global economy operates without the crises that lead to unemployment, social misery and disturbances.

One may develop an understanding at the macro level by basing it on the principles stated in the previous chapters. However, since the firm was the unit of analysis in those chapters, one cannot simply use the same considerations and factors. If a theory of the macro level is to have any chance of being empirically tested, it has to be distinct and not too complicated. In the next chapter I will therefore develop a model which will be based on the foregoing analysis.

188 *The Strategic Management of Innovation*

However, I will go further than that, and formalize the factors and considerations. This means that new factors and factor relations will be introduced. Here the theory breaks away more from the empirical foundation that formed the point of departure for the foregoing micro analysis. The discussion moves from what Glaser and Strauss (1970) call substantial theory (discursive conclusions of empirical analyses) to formal theory (formally formulated models, less tied to the empirical material).

The next chapter thus offers a model of the innovation process that can be used to analyse the innovation capacity of an industry, a nation or any other larger societal unit. The model specifies which factors in which relations are supposed to determine innovative firm behaviour and thus the economic development of the unit. At this stage the model is purely theoretical and needs empirical testing to be fully valid. However, that is the way it is with theoretical models.

The model concerns only innovation processes. Although general sociological considerations will be included in the discussion in this chapter, this is not a general theory of social change. It is a theory of that part of social change which is created by the market mechanism. This is not only material change. For example, it includes innovation in services. As has been argued in the previous chapters, services are widely distributed by the market mechanism, and services concern our feelings, well-being and intellectual capacity.

Above, I claimed that the model will cover economic development. This is correct, understood within the Schumpeterian tradition. However, it could be objected that not all economic development is created through innovation and the market mechanism; political interventions may also create such development. This may be true in the sense that the model will not cover all economic development, but only market-based development. The model explains innovation and organizational learning in firms as a system of economic and social change.

In this chapter, before I present the model, I will elaborate the principle for developing a macro model – a process which has already been started – and placing it in an evolutionary framework.

2 THE MODEL AS AN EVOLUTIONARY INNOVATION SYSTEM

2.1 The Evolutionary Framework

The model has so far been kept within an evolutionary framework (cf. Metcalfe 1998). The evolutionary approach used here is, however, not the 'hard' one, but a 'soft' one, as stated in Chapter 3. The idea is not that a hard selection mechanism exists, which may be found and used to predict future development. Within this framework one might not even be able to explain which firms will survive and why (as, for example, stated by the organizational population ecology theory of Hannan and Freeman 1989). It may in principle be possible to answer the second question (the 'why'), but this would require an enormous amount of analytical work.

The 'soft' version used here is analogous to biological ecological systems characterized by chaos. The individual elements of the system are interrelated in highly complex ways, with many factors influencing each other through several intermediate links. This does not mean that the system is anarchistic and completely without order. It means that the order is very complex.

The model thus presents a series of factors that influence innovation. They do so within micro systems, and their overall determination of the societal innovation process is impossible to describe in such a model. The configuration of the influencing factors varies from one societal system to another, and within the same system from time to time. The usefulness of the model is that it can help us to identify innovation-determining factors that can be influenced (for example by industrial policy, labour market policy and educational policy) even though one cannot predict what will happen to the overall innovation system.

2.2   The Model as a Social Change Model

The formulation of the model represents a re-introduction of the social change theory (LaPiere 1965; Moore 1963; Etzioni and Etzioni 1964), which was also a macro model. This theory too was based on innovation as the foundation of social change. However, the model in the next chapter has a more limited scope. As pointed out, it concerns social changes that are determined via the market or market-like systems such as the public service delivery system. It is not a theory of general social change. Factors other than innovation and systems other than the market (for example, ideologies and political actions) create social change.

Nor is the model an expression of the functionalistic view that characterized much of the social change literature of the 1950s and 1960s (typically Moore 1963, 1967); nor will I claim that all market-based changes and all innovations emerge because they have a function, nor that they are all useful to society. This 'soft' evolutionary approach is not based on a postulated progress where each innovation will bring greater happiness to mankind. Some innovations present new solutions to some problems and are thus useful. Others create more problems than they solve. Others again are just useless or 'for fun'. Even though innovation as a phenomenon might create problems and be useless, it also solves problems and creates social and economic welfare. This is the reason for dealing with ways in which the innovation process in society can be improved. The model here is a general model; it does not go into depth about the types of innovation that should be developed – for example, whether a new product might create ecological problems, or a new organizational form might create psychological and social problems among employees. The ethical and functional problems are left to other analyses, which does not mean that these problems should not be addressed – only that this is not possible within the limits and scope of this book.

2.3   The Model as a Basis for Political Intervention

Even if one excludes ethical and functional problems, there is an issue of political intervention on which one must take a position. Economic and industrial policy exists, and is an attempt to create economic growth and solve economic, social and functional problems. An innovation model for a society is not only a tool for understanding; it sets the scene for industrial policy. Governments and other political authorities may want to intervene to improve innovation capacity and economic development. I will therefore briefly discuss here the type of policy for which the future model and its basis set the scene.

A possible policy based on this model would be like the model itself: strategic and interactive. One cannot single out a limited number of factors that might be influenced, and thus deterministically predict the direction of economic development and how much innovation will be created. It will be a process where many things can happen, among other reasons because other players will react to the intervention. For example, intervention that improves some factors and gives an advantage to some firms could prompt other firms to react by developing other factors. These may even be conservative, non-innovative factors, yet they might lead to success. This is the essence of the strategic innovation theory – that firms act as participants in a strategic game.

Any political intervention also has to be strategic. The intervening authority has to make an analysis in order to select the factors that seem most important. It must then try to influence them, follow developments, analyse them and perhaps change the policy.

The strategic character of the innovation system has recently been reflected in industrial policy, at least within the European Union (Borras 2001). In European countries and in the European Commission, industrial policy has shifted from a focus on technology promotion to the creation of general frameworks that improve the firms' potential for developing on their own premises. These frameworks will be different for different types of firms. The scene is left to the interactive strategic process.

3 THE MODEL AS AN EXPLANATION OF ECONOMIC DEVELOPMENT

The model can be said to explain an innovation system in a society (or an industry, or whatever the unit is). The economic development of the society is the combined result of the innovation activities of many firms. This is the idea of the evolutionary economic approach. The problem is how one defines 'system' and how one explains the determination mechanism of the system.

3.1 The Model Describes Innovation Systems

The term 'system' has been used to describe interrelated innovation factors within a unit (a nation, a region and so on). Some theories have talked about national systems of innovation (Nelson 1993, Lundvall 1992) as flows of knowledge between firms and other actors, and general innovation projects. It is assumed that the firms learn from one other. This is, however, a fairly rational tradition, even though it has claimed to represent a more complex understanding and has included sociological factors, unlike neoclassical economics. Knowledge flows, learning processes and innovation projects are considered fairly rational. This view is also expressed in Nelson and Winter's evolutionary theory of economic development (Nelson and Winter 1982). They focus on routines as the one fundamental factor that can explain economic development. Other attempts are based on knowledge, competencies or learning as the one fundamental factor that can explain economic development and which can be measured simply (cf. Chapter 4).

The strategic innovation theory is more complex, less deterministic and thus not as rationalistic as the tradition mentioned above, although to some degree it is based on that tradition. It involves more variables and more relations among the variables, and it cannot be reduced to one fundamental explanatory factor. The system is more 'loosely coupled' than others (cf. Sundbo and Gallouj 2000). The theory is based on a sociological view combined with a strategic approach. Actors are determinants in the system because they decide where to go, and theyestablish a strategy. They may go their own ways – although they may have a tendency to follow the same pattern of behaviour as other actors (this is the foundation for the existence of sociology as a science). They are driven by strategic reflexivity (Sundbo and Fuglsang 2001). Each actor in this system may be defined as a firm. However, these firms interact with one another, not only by forging alliances and creating networks, but also by competing and by creating smarter strategies than their competitors. Furthermore, within each firm the innovation process is driven by individuals who also act within an interaction system. If one were to identify a core characteristic of, or factor in, the strategic innovation theory, and thus the proposed model, it would be interactionism.

3.2 The Interaction Economy

The model is an explanation of economic development. Innovations create economic growth. They further contribute to the development of a general growth system, for example by developing organizational forms that are efficient tools for developing innovations. A high level of innovativeness within firms (high innovation stock and capability and good management capacity) in a country creates better potential for future innovations. This second-order level of an innovation system is the reason for using the term 'economic development' rather than just 'economic growth': there is more to it than simple growth. In his classic work Schumpeter (1934) used the term 'economic development'.

4   A MODEL OF INDIVIDUAL AND INTERACTION VARIABLES

The model is not simplistic, as mentioned above when it was discussed in relation to theories of economic development. It presents a series of factors, dimensions and relations that can be measured, for example within a country. This may seem like McClelland's (1961) attempt to measure a country's innovative capability or Hagen's (1962) attempt to do the same. The system of setting up a series of variables that can measure a society's innovative capability is the same, but there is a difference from McClelland's variables. His model has a psychological aim and is based purely on entrepreneurship theory, which means that his variables are directed towards explaining individual behaviour.

This model has a sociological aim, and is meant to explain the behaviour of collective social systems such as firms and groups. Interaction plays a greater role. This also means that the model is based on relations and scales which describe the distance between two characteristics. The dimensions of the model relate to interactions. However, the model also includes several individual-oriented dimensions. Entrepreneurship plays a role in the strategic innovation theory, but not as central a role as in McClelland's or Hagen's theories.

17.   A Model of the Innovation System

In this chapter I will present and discuss the model, as promised in Chapter 16. First I will discuss the innovation determinants to which the strategic innovation theory leads. These determinants are general, specifying the factors that are important in understanding the innovation process. Next I will present some submodels that specify more precisely the dimensions that improve the system's innovative capability. These submodels elaborate parts of the general determinant model presented first, and thus deepen our understanding of the innovation system.

The determinants and dimensions have been chosen because they represent the interaction economy. This choice takes us a step further away from the empirical basis of the previous part of the book. A more pure theoretical approach always involves some personal selection, and this one is no exception.. Still, the proof lies in the subsequent empirical investigation.

1 INNOVATION DETERMINANTS

How can interaction patterns and strategic management be explained? What are the basic determinants of these phenomena? This will be discussed in this section.

The basic factor is human resources, that is, the ability to create innovation processes. This requires that individuals and the firm as organization have certain characteristics. Since we are at the macrolevel here, we are interested in these characteristics as ones of a nation (or whatever definition of society one is dealing with – it might be a regional or supranational organization like the European Union, for example).

1.1 The Human Determinants of Innovation

The following characteristics are the important determinants at the individual level.

Individual Characteristics

- *Entrepreneurship.* The drive to realize one's ideas and become a powerful and prestigious person. Action-orientation. The traditional entrepreneurship characteristics (cf. Sexton and Kasarda 1992).
- *Creativity.* This means the ability to see new solutions. It includes the action-orientation that characterizes the classic entrepreneur, but not in an extreme form. Since the innovation process is interactive, too much self-assertion and individual action may destroy the process.
- *Interactiveness.* The ability and willingness to communicate ideas and interact with other people. This includes the ability to put oneself in the place of others and understand their situation, needs and ideas.
- *Learning ability.* Learning is not only a question of appropriating external knowledge or information, but also of relating this to one's own existing knowledge and experience and creating new knowledge from this combination of elements.

Managers must also have some characteristics, which are as follows.

Management Characteristics

- *Ability to 'read' the environment.* Managers must be able to foresee what will happen in the market and in society in the future. This primarily requires awareness of the future possibilities, which is a particular personal characteristic. It also requires that managers have some methods for looking into the future.
- *Ability to formulate persuasive strategies.* Managers should be able to formulate strategies, and this too requires that they are able to employ certain methods. They should also be able to get employees to follow the strategy. This requires some charisma, but not too much, because that would kill the employees' initiative. A society cannot depend on top entrepreneurs; they are too rare and too dangerous.
- *Ability to balance innovation processes.* Managers should be able to inspire employees to innovate but at the same time be able to restrict innovation. The difficulty is to get employees to accept both.
- *Managers should be able to organize successful project teams.* This is to a great extent a question of experience and formal methods.
- *Alliance-building.* Forming alliances with external actors is important. It requires open-mindedness, a persuasive character and a certain shrewdness.

It is not only individual characteristics that are crucial; organizational culture characteristics are equally important. Norms for how one interacts and behaves within groups may vary among countries and cultural regions. Organizational culture characteristics are viewed here at the societal level (not the level of the individual firm). The following organizational characteristics are important.

Organizational Characteristics

- *Self-manifestation.* That is, the extent to which it is accepted that the individual may manifest himself in the organization. There must be norms which allow individuals to show openly that they are career-minded, power-seeking and competition-oriented. However, this characteristic should not be too extreme.
- *Interactivity.* One important cultural element is a tradition for cooperation and taking care of other people. This will improve interaction, can lead to idea creation and learning, and it will improve project team efficiency.
- *Role pluralism.* The culture should have a tradition for permitting the different roles that are necessary in the interactive innovation process. These may be roles such as analyst, entrepreneur, 'leader' (someone who can make others follow him), coordinator, critic and so on.
- *Networking.* A tradition for openness towards the outside world is important. This means a tradition for building a network out of one's own group (in this case the organization of the firm). This requires fundamental trust in other people, but also some caution and scepticism so that people will not be disappointed too much.

These are the important determinants of the innovation process and thus of economic development.

1.2 The Determinants are Culturally Based

These determinants come from the educational system of the society. The concept of educational system is used in a broad sense here. It includes the socialization that takes place in childhood and the social and cultural developments that take place in society and which may change the cultural heritage that the educational system has produced.

The extended education system includes: (1) Socialization in families; (2) The school system; (3)Internal development in enterprises; and (4) The societal culture (for example, awareness of innovation, whether norms are change-actuating etc.).

The aspects of the cultural education system that are important are not only personal characteristics such as those McClelland (1961) investigated in his attempt to measure national entrepreneurship levels, they also include interaction patterns. McClelland wanted to measure classic entrepreneurship, not the kind of interactive, collective entrepreneurship I am talking about here. The cultural aspects spoken of here are more like those Hofstede (1980, 1991) has measured, although his parameters do not quite match those that are relevant here.

The general abilities necessary are that people are good at functioning in collective group settings, but also at deciding, taking their own course and struggling to achieve their goals.

1.3 Auxiliary Factors

There are also some auxiliary factors which are not direct determinants, but which are necessary inputs for the innovation process. Here we find some of the traditional innovation factors. The auxiliary factors are as follows.

- *Knowledge*. Knowledge in the form of existing information is a necessary input factor. Knowledge development may follow certain trajectories, as described in earlier chapters. However, knowledge does not produce innovation in itself, only through the minds and interactions of individuals.
- *Technology development*. New technology provides new possibilities for innovation. However, it only provides just that – possibilities. A fundamental premise of the strategic innovation theory is that the strategy leads the innovation process which is implemented by the dual organization. A certain technology will only be adopted if it fits into the innovation plans. Its existence alone will not force the firm to introduce it.
- *R&D activities*. These are also important inputs in innovation processes. However, again they do not determine the innovations: the strategy and the dual organization including managers' decisions do that. R&D departments are important players in the innovation process, but there are other players as well.
- *Information and communication technology networks*. These networks are becoming increasingly important as a means of procuring knowledge, that is, the input in the innovation process, and of creating and distributing innovations (for example, in services). It may be assumed that the more efficient and widespread networks are in a nation (an industry, a region or other), the better its potential for a high degree of innovation.
- *Other trajectories and actors*. These were defined in Figure 7.1. Such external trajectories and actors are important input factors in the innovation

process, but it is still the management and the internal interaction system that decide upon innovations.

1.4 Balance between Psychological and Cultural Variables

How does one measure the core innovation determinants? The list of variables above is long and the variables are fairly abstract. A more operational model is needed. A few psychological and cultural variables should be set up to create a handy model. This will be done in this section. The model must also give some degree of explanation – which variables and how much of each will result in innovation and thus economic development?

A model will be presented in this section. The principle here will be balance. My empirical innovation studies have taught me that the interactive innovation process is most efficient when it has different, sometimes opposing, characteristics in a balanced setting (Sundbo 1996). Thus rational innovation behaviour – which is an economic factor (in that it creates economic growth) – is a complex pattern of social phenomena.

We are here talking about innovativeness at the macro – national or industrial – level. This macro innovativeness consists of a combination of these social or psychological phenomena among the population of the chosen universe.

2 DIMENSIONS OF INNOVATIVENESS

I will here propose a model with certain dimensions that I consider, on the basis of my empirical research, to be the most important. They will be presented as pairs of psychological variables which characterize individuals. However, these variables are results of the cultural process in society, as described above.

2.1 Balance between Entrepreneurial Selfishness and Interactive Sociability

The optimal innovation behaviour is achieved if characteristics from both ends of the scale are present. The optimum is somewhere in the middle of each dimension. However, at this theoretical level it is impossible to say exactly where the optimal point is – whether it is exactly in the middle or to one or the other side of the middle.

The essence of the model is a balance between selfishness and sociability, with a dynamic drive in both: selfishness with a drive to realize one's ideas and gain personal power and status, like the drive of the entrepreneur; and sociability with a drive to develop new solutions in a collective setting and at the same time take care of the other members of the collectivity – team spirit.

This is expressed in the five dimensions of figure 17.1.

Figure 17.1   Five dimensions of strategic, interactive innovation

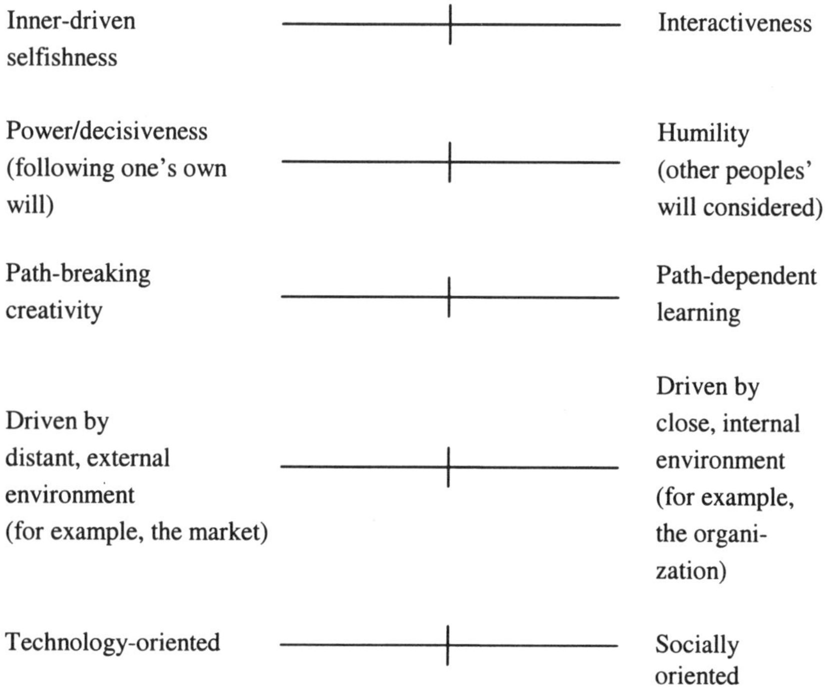

Inner-driven selfishness	————————┼————————	Interactiveness
Power/decisiveness (following one's own will)	————————┼————————	Humility (other peoples' will considered)
Path-breaking creativity	————————┼————————	Path-dependent learning
Driven by distant, external environment (for example, the market)	————————┼————————	Driven by close, internal environment (for example, the organization)
Technology-oriented	————————┼————————	Socially oriented

If one were to decide empirically on the optimal composition of these dimensions and the optimal point in each of them, one would need to make time studies in enterprises. Each person has a little of each characteristics and may exercise it to different extents in different roles within the firm. One would have to follow many individuals throughout the day and note when they exercise which characteristics, and sum all this up at an industrial, regional or national level. This would involve quite another kind of data than the usual statistics.

2.2 An Optimal Economic Model of Innovativeness in Society

One could express the general selfishness–sociability dimension in relation to the dynamicCstatic dimension. In an evolutionary perspective, dynamism and staticism may be supposed to be in balance. Not many contemporary societies are either purely static or extremely dynamic without stable elements. One can assume that a society will seek an optimal condition midway along the selfishness–sociability dimension – which produces an optimal degree of entrepreneurship – and close to, but not quite at, the dynamic end of the dynamic–static dimension.

The model may be expressed as shown in figure 17.2.

Figure 17.2   Optimal model of innovativeness in society

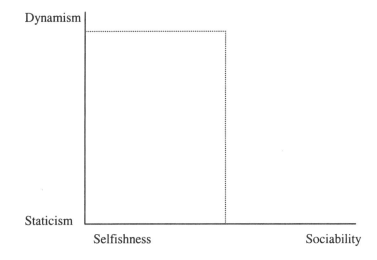

2.3 Distribution of Innovative Roles

Individuals exhibit certain behaviour – and thus psychological characteristics – through their roles in the enterprise organization. The different psychological traits can be summarized in terms of three main roles that are crucial to the innovation process. These roles can be found in empirical research (cf. Sundbo 1998a, where the interactor role is not indicated, however). The roles are as follows:

- entrepreneur (action-oriented);
- analyst (knowledge-oriented); and
- interactor (interaction-oriented).

All of these roles are important to strategic, interactive innovation behaviour. They are not individual or personalities in the sense that each member of society occupies one or the other of the roles. Most individuals play several roles at different times of the day or in their lives. Thus the roles characterize general social behaviour in the society.

The three roles form a triangle, as shown in Figure 17.3e:

Figure 17.3   Innovative roles

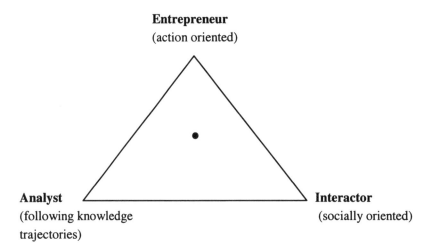

An equal distribution of the roles would be the optimum for an innovation system – a nation, an industry or whatever. This is the centre of the triangle. However, a specific system may have its empirical middle point elsewhere.

The three sides of the triangle express three extreme types of innovative system. Probably no country, industry or other unit will have any of these extreme innovation systems in a pure form – there will always be a mix. These extreme innovation systems are expressed in Figure 17.4.

Figure 17.4   Innovation systems

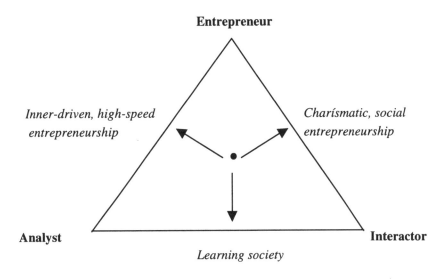

Each of the three extreme innovation systems in its pure form is non-optimal:

Inner-driven, high-speed entrepreneurship is the American ideal – the individual who can analyse the possibilities on the market and who can act and struggle. However, he will rarely be able to carry the whole innovation process through by himself in contemporary society. This requires cooperation with other people, something this type is not good at, so the innovation processes will often fail in the late phases. There may be cultural differences, but even in the United States this system will not be optimal without the other systems represented.

Social entrepreneurship is charismatic change making which can get people following it. It may come close to the ideal, but it may create some difficulties in learning and knowledge creation and also inhibit more radical innovation. It has a tendency to become preoccupied with motivation, involvement and other social processes that are not necessarily innovative.

The learning society stores only information and learning. It is not very suited to action. It has too great an aversion to risk, because of a tendency to base all action on solid knowledge. It lacks the 'wild' trial-and-error actions of the entrepreneur.

3 LEARNING CAPACITY

The learning capacity of a society is also the result of a balance between firms' ability to absorb external knowledge and to combine it with their own knowledge, including the tacit kind (cf. Polanyi 1966). External knowledge is generally formal and follows the trajectories described in Chapter 7, but useful tacit knowledge exists outside these trajectories. Internal knowledge is based on practical experience ('theory-in-use' as Argyris and Schön 1978 call it) and is partly formalized, partly tacit (cf. Nonaka and Takeuchi 1995).

Thus neither a purely formal knowledge trajectory nor the purely tacit knowledge existing within organizations is sufficient. The balance is expressed in Figure 17.5 (compared with the ones above).

Figure 17.5   Balance of learning capacity

Absorption of external knowledge ———————————— Firm-internal knowledge

The absorption of external knowledge is generally a one-way type of communication, while the development and use of internal knowledge is normally an interactive process. That is why this process is the most important one, even when we are talking about formal and trajectorial external knowledge. It must be dealt with in an interactive process in order to become learning. External and internal knowledge are combined, a creative element is added, and it is all developed into new, action-oriented knowledge.

A country's innovation capability (through its learning capacity) depends on the existence of both types of knowledge, obtaining the right balance between these forms of knowledge, and the ability to combine different learning elements – and is thus a quite complicated process, which is not easy to measure.

Bibliography

Abernathy, W.J. and Utterback, J.M. (1978), Patterns of Industrial Innovations, *Technological Review* vol. 80 no, 7, June pp. 2–29.

Ackoff, R.L. (1981), *Creating the Corporate Future*, New York (Wiley).

Alexander, M. (1992), Brief Case: Strategic Fatigue, *Long Range Planning*, vol. 25, no. 2, pp. 119–21.

Andersen, E.S. (1996), *Evolutionary Economics – Post-Schumpeterian Contributions*, London (Pinter).

Ansoff, H.N. (1965), *Corporate Strategy*, New York (McGraw-Hill).

Ansoff, H.N. (1988), *The New Corporate Strategy*, New York (Wiley).

Argyris, C. (1965), *Organization and Innovation*, Homewood Ill. (Irwin).

Argyris, C. (1992), *On Organizational Learning*, Cambridge Mass. (Blackwell).

Argyris, C. and Schön, D. (1978), *Organizational Learning: A Theory of Action Perspective*, Reading Mass. (Addison-Wesley).

Baker, M. (1985), *Marketing Strategy and Management*, London (Macmillan).

Barney, J. (1991), Firm Resources and Sustained Competitive Advantage, *Journal of Management*, vol. 17, no. 1, pp. 99–120.

Berger, P and Luckmann, T. (1966), *The Social Construction of Reality*,

Bevort, F., Sundbo, J. and Pedersen, J.S. (1992), HRM in Denmark – Recent Trends, *Employee Relations*, vol. 14, no. 4, pp. 6–20.

Bevort, F., Pedersen, J.S. and Sundbo, J. (1995), Human resource Management in Denmark; in Brunstein, I. (ed.), *Human Resource Management in Europe*, Berlin (De Gruyter).

Bijker, W. Hughes, T. and Pinch, T. (1987), *The Social Construction of Technological Systems*, Cambridge Mass. (MIT Press).

Binswanger, H.P. et. al. (1978*), Induced Innovation*, Baltimore (John Hopkins University Press).

Borras, S. (2001), Recent Trends of EU Innovation Policy: A New Context for Strategic Reflexivity, in Sundbo, J. and Fuglsang, L., *Innovation as Strategic Reflexivity,* London (Routledge) (forthcoming).

Burgelman, R.A. and Sayles, L.R. (1986), *Inside Corporate Innovation: Strategy, Structure and Managerial Skills*, New York (Free Press).

Burns, T. and Stalker, G.M. (1961), *The Management of Innovation*, London (Tavistock).

Chaffee, E. (1985), Three Models of Strategy, *Management Review*, vol. 10, no. 1. pp. 89–98.

Chandler, A.D. (1990), *Scale and Scope*, Cambridge Mass. (Belknap).

Christensen, J.F. (1996), Innovation assets and inter-asset linkages – A resource-based approach to innovation, *Economic Innovation and New Technology*, vol. 4, pp. 193-209.

Coase, R.H. (1937), The Nature of the Firm, *Economica*, 4, pp. 386–405.

Coombs, R., Saviotti, P. and Walsh, V. (1987), *Economics and Technological Change*, London (Macmillan)

Cooper, R.G. (1988), *Winning at New Products*, Ontario (Addison-Wesley).

Daft, R. (1978), A Dual-Core Model of Organizational Innovation, *Academy of Management Journal*, vol. 21, no. 2, pp. 193-210.

Dahmén, E. (1986), Schumpeterian Dynamics, in Day, R. and Eliasson, G. (eds), *The Dynamics of Market Economics*, Amsterdam (North Holland).

Davenport, T. (1993), *Process Innovation*, Boston (Harvard Business School Press).

Dodgson, M. (1993), Organizational Learning: A Review of Some Literature, *Organization Studies*, vol. 14, no. 3, pp. 375–94.

Donaldson, L. (1996), The Normal Science of Structural Contingency Theory, in Clegg, S. Hardy, C and Nord, W. (eds.), *Handbook of Organization Studies*, London (Sage).

Dosi, G. (1982), Technological Paradigms and Technological Trajectories: A Suggested Interpretation of the Determinants and Directions of Technical Change, *Research Policy*, vol. 2, no.3, pp. 147–62.

Dosi, G., Freeman, C., Nelson, R., Silverberg, G. and Soete, L. (eds.) (1988), *Technical Change and Economic Theory*, London (Pinter).

Drucker, P. (1985), *Innovation and Entrepreneurship*, New York (Harper & Row).

Drucker, P. (1993), *Post-capitalist Society*, Oxford (Butterworth-Heinemann)

Duijn, J. van (1984), Fluctuations in Innovations over Time, in Freeman, C.

Duus, H.J. (1997), Economic Foundation for an Entrepreneurial Marketing Concept, *Scandinavian Journal of Management* vol. 13, no. 3, pp. 287–305.

Eiglier, P. and Langeard, E. (1988), *Servuction*, Paris (McGraw-Hill).

Eliasson, G. (1989), The Dynamics of Supply and Economic Growth – How Industrial Knowledge Accumulation Drives a Path–Dependent Economic Process, in Carlsson, B. (ed.), *Industrial Dynamics*, Boston (Kluwer Academics).

Etzioni, A. and Etzioni, E. (1964), *Social Change*, New York (Basic Books).

Foss, N.J. (1993), Theories of the Firm: Contractual and Competence Perspectives, *Journal of Evolutionary Economics*, vol. 3, no. 2, pp. 127–44

Foss, N.J. (1994), *Capabilities and the Competitive Advantage of Nations: Some Conceptual Suggestions*, Paper 94-7 from Institute of Industrial Economics and Strategy, Copenhagen Business School, Copenhagen.

Foss, N.J. (ed.) (1997), *Resources, Firms and Strategies*, Oxford (Oxford University Press).

Foucault, M. (1980), *Power/Knowledge*, Brighton (Harvester).

Freeman, C. (1974), *The Economics of Industrial Innovation*, London (Pinter).

Freeman, C. (ed.) (1984), *Long Waves in the World Economy*, London (Pinter).

Freeman, C. and Perez, C. (1988), Structural Crisis of Adjustment: Business Cycles and Investment Behavior, in Dosi, G. et. al.

Freeman, C. and Soete, L. (1997), *The Economics of Industrial Innnovation*, London (Pinter).

Gadrey, J., Gallouj, F., Lhuillery, S., Weinstein. O. and Ribault, T. (1993), *Etude effectuée pour le ministère de l'enseignement superieur et de la recherche* (working papers from project for Ministry of Education and Research on innovation in service), Lille (IFRESI-CNRS, Université des sciences et technologies de Lille):
Lhuillery, S., *La recherche-développement dans les services en France: une étude statistique.*
Gadrey, J. and Gallouj, F., *La recherche-développement et l'innovation dans le secteur des compagnies d'assurance: Synthèse sectorielle et études de cas.*
Weinstein, O., Lhuillery, S. and Ribault, T., *La recherche-développement et l'innovation dans le secteur des services d'information electronique: Synthèse sectorielle et études de cas.*
Gallouj, F., *La recherche-développement et l'innovation dans le secteur de conseil aux enterprises: Synthèse sectorielles et études de cas.*
Lhuillery, S. *La recherche-développement et l'innovation bancaire: Etudes de cas.*
Gadrey, J., Gallouj, F., Lhuillery, S. and Weinstein, O., *Les critères définissant l'activité de recherche-développement et les cas des entreprises de services.*

Gallouj, F. (1994a), *Économie de l'innovation dans les services*, Paris (Harmattan).

Gallouj, F. (1997), Towards a Neo-Schumpeterian Theory of Innovation in services?, *Science and Public Policy*, vol. 24, no. 6, pp. 405–20.

Giddens, A. (1984), *The Constitution of Society*, Oxford (Policy).

Glaser, B.G. and Strauss, A.L. (1970), *The Discovery of Grounded Theory. Strategies for Qualitative Research*, Chicago (Aldine) .

Grant, R. (1991), The Resource–Based Theory of Competitive Advantage: Implications for Strategy Formulation, *California Management Review*, Spring, pp. 114–35.

Grønhaug, K. and Nordhaug, O (1992), Strategy and Competence in Firms, *European Management Journal*, vol. 10, no. 4, pp. 438–44.

Grönroos, C. (1990), *Service Management and Marketing: Managing the Moments of Truth in Service Competition*, Lexington (Lexington Books).

Gummesson, E. (1999), *Total Relationship Marketing*, Oxford (Butterworth-Heinemann).

Hage, J. (1980), *Theories of Organizations*, New York (Wiley).

Hagen, E. E. (1962), *On the Theory of Social Change*, Homewood Ill. (Dorsey).

Håkansson, H. (ed.) (1987), *Industrial Technology Development. A Network Approach*, London (Routledge).

Hamel, G. and Prahalad, C.K. (1994), *Competing for the Future*, Boston (Harvard Business School Press).

Hammer, M. and Champy, J. (1993), *Reengineering the Corporation*, London (Nicholas Brealey).

Hannan, M. and Freeman, J. (1989), *Organizational Ecology*, Cambridge (Harvard University Press).

Haukness, J. (1998), *Services in Innovation – Innovation in Services*, SI4S final report, STEP group, Oslo (STEP group).

Heap, J.P. (1989), *The Management of Innovation and Design*, London (Cassell).

Hippel, E. von (1988), *The Sources of Innovation*, Oxford (Oxford University Press).

Hodgson, G. (1988), *Economics and Institutions*, Cambridge (Polity).

Hodgson, G. (1998), Competence and Contract in the Theory of the Firm, *Journal of Economic Behavior and Organization*, vol. 35, p. 179–201.

Hofstede, G. (1980), *Culture's Consequences*, London (Sage).

Hofstede, G. (1991), *Culture and Organizations*, London (McGraw-Hill).

Horwitch, M. (ed.) (1985), Special Issue: Technology in the Modern Corporation. A Strategic Perspective, *Technology in Society*, vol. 7, no. 2/3.

Hübner, H. (ed.) (1986), *The Art and Science of Innovation Management*, Amsterdam (Elsevier).

Illeris, S. (1996), *The Service Economy. A Geographical Approach*, Chichester (Wiley).

Johannisson, B. (1988), Business Formation – A Network Approach, *Scandinavian Journal of Management*, vol. 4, no. 3/4, pp. 83–99.

Kamien, M. and Schwartz, N.L. (1982), *Market Structure and Innovation*, Cambridge (Cambridge University Press).

Kanter, R.M. (1983), *The Change Masters*, London (Unwin).

Kanter, R.M. (1989), *When the Giants Learn to Dance*, London (Routledge).

Kirzner, I. (1973), *Competition and Entrepreneurship*, Chicago (University of Chicago Press).

Kline, S. (1985), Innovation Is Not a Linear Process, *Research Management*, vol. 28, no. 4, pp. 36-45.

Kline, S. and Rosenberg, N. (1986), An Overview of Innovation, in Landau, R. and Rosenberg, N. (eds.), *The Positive Sum Strategy: Harnessing Technology for Economic Growth*, Washington DC (National Academy Press).

Knights, D. and Morgan, G. (1995), Strategy under the Microscope: Strategic Management and IT in Finacial Services, *Journal of Management Studies*, vol. 32, no. 2, pp. 191–214.

Kondratiev, N.D. (1935), The Long Waves in Economic Life, *Review of Economic Statistics*, vol. 17 no. 6 pp. 105–15.

Kotler, P. (1983), *Principles of Marketing*, Englewood Cliffs (Prentice Hall).

LaPiere, R.T. (1965), *Social Change*, New York (McGraw-Hill).

Lawrence, P.R. and Lorsch, J.W. (1967), *Organization and Environment*, Cambridge Mass. (Graduate School of Business Administration, Harvard University).

Lipietz, A. (1987), *Mirages and Miracles. The Crisis of Global Fordism*, London (Verso).

Lundberg, G., Schrag, C. and Larsen, O. (1963), *Sociology*, New York (Harper & Row).

Lundvall, B.-Å. (1988), Innovation as an Interactive Process: From User-Producer Interaction to the National System of Innovation, in Dosi, G. et. al.

Lundvall, B.-Å. (ed.) (1992), *National Systems of Innovation*, London (Pinter).

Lundvall, B.Å. and Foray, D. (1996), The Knowledge-Based Economy, in *Employment and growth in the knowledge-based economy*, OECD Document, Paris (OECD).

Lyotard, J.-F. (1984), *The Post-Modern Condition*, Manchester (Manchester University Press).

Machlup, F. (1983), *Knowledge and Knowledge Production*, Princeton (Princeton University Press).

Majaro, S. (1988), *The Creative Gap*, London (Longman).

March, J. and Simon, P. (1958), *Organizations*, New York (Wiley).

Mattsson, J. (1993), Improving Service Quality in Person-to-Person Encounters, *The Service Industries Journal*, vol. 14, no. 1, pp. 45–61.

Mattsson, J. (1994), Quality Blueprints of Internal Producer Services, *International Journal of Service Industry Management*, vol. 4, no. 4, pp. 66–80.

McClelland, D. (1961), *The Achieving Society*, Princeton (van Nostrand).

Mead, G.H. (1934), *Mind, Self and Society*, Chicago (University of Chicago Press).

Metcalfe, S. (1998), *Evolutionary Economics and Creative Destruction*, London (Routledge).

Meyer, M. and Roberts, E. (1986), New Product Strategy in Small Technology–Based Firms: A Pilot Study, *Management Science* vol. 32, no. 7, pp. 806–21.

Miles, I. (1993), Services in the New Industrial Ecocony, *Futures*, vol. 25, July/August, pp. 653–72.

Miles, I., Kastrinos, N., Flanagan, K., Bilderbek, R., den Hertog, P., Huntink, W. and Bouman, M. (1994), *Knowledge-Intensive Business Services: Their Role as Users, Carriers and Sources of Innovation*, Manchester (PREST, University of Manchester, Manchester).

Mintzberg, H. (1979), *The Structuring of Organizations*, Englewood Cliffs (Prentice Hall).

Mintzberg, H. (1989), *Mintzberg on Management*, New York (Free Press).

Mintzberg, H. (1994), *The Rise and Fall of Strategic Planning*, New York (Free Press).

Mintzberg, H. and McHughes, A. (1985), Strategy Formation in an AdHocracy, *Administrative Science Quarterly*, vol. 30, no. 2, pp.160–97.

Mintzberg, H. and Waters, J. (1982), Tracking Strategy in an Entrepreneurial Firm, *Academy of Management Journal*, vol. 25, no. 3, pp. 465–99.

Moore, W.E. (1963), *Social Change*, Englewood Cliffs (Prentice-Hall).

Moore, W.E. (1967), *Order and Change*, New York (Wiley).

Nelson, R. (ed.) (1993), *National Innovation Systems*, Oxford (Oxford University Press).

Nelson, R. and Winter, S.G. (1982), *An Evolutionary Theory of Economic Change*, Cambridge Mass. (Belknap).

Nonaka, I. and Takeuchi, H. (1995), *The Knowledge-Creating Company*, Oxford (Oxford University Press).

Normann, R. (1991), *Service Management*, 2nd ed., Chichester UK (Wiley).

Nyström, H. (1979), *Creativity and Innovation*, Chichester (Wiley).

Nyström, H. (1990), *Technological and Market Innovation*, Chichester (Wiley).

OECD (1996), *Employment and Growth in the Kknowledge-based Economy*, OECD Document, Paris (OECD).

Penrose, E.T. (1959), *The Theory of the Growth of the Firm*, New York (Blackwell).

Perez, C. (1983), Structural Change and the Assimilation of New Technologies in the Economic and Social System, *Futures*, vol. 15, no. 4, pp. 357–75.

Peters, T.J. and Waterman, R.H. (1982), *In Search of Excellence*, New York (Harper & Row).

Pettigrew, A. (1985), *The Awakening Giant. Continuity and Change at ICI*, Oxford (Blackwell).

Phillips, A. (1971), *Technology and Market Structure*, Lexington (Lexington Books).

Pinchot, G. (1985), *Intrapreneuring*, New York (Harper & Row).

Pine, B.J. (1993), *Mass Customization*, Boston (Harvard Business School Press).

Piore, M.J. and Sabel, C.F. (1984), *The Second Industrial Divide*, New York (Basic Books).

Polanyi, M (1966), *The Tacit Dimension*, London (Routledge & Kegan Paul).

Porter, M. (1980), *Competitive Strategy*, New York (Free Press).

Porter, M. (1985), *Competitive Advantage*, New York (Free Press).

Porter, M. (1990), *The Competitive Advantage of Nations*, New York (Macmillan).

Prigogine, I. and Stengers, I. (1984), *Order out of Chaos: Man's New Dialogue with Nature*, London (Heineman).

Quinn, J.B. (1992), *Intelligent Enterprise*, New York (Free Press).

Reich, R. (1991), *The Work of Nations*, New York (Simon and Schuster).

Rogers, E.M. (1995), *Diffusion of Innovation*, New York (Free Press) (2nd edition).

Rosenberg, N. (1976), *Perspectives on Technology*, Cambridge Mass. (Cambridge University Press).

Rosenberg, N. (1982), *Inside the Black Box*, Cambridge Mass. (Cambridge University Press).

Rumelt, R.P. (1984), Towards a Strategic Theory of the Firm, in Lamb, R.B. (ed.), *Competitive Strategic Management*, Englewood Cliffs (Prentice-Hall).

Schein, E. (1984), *Organizational Culture and Leadership*, San Francisco (Jossey-Bass).

Schmookler, H. (1966), *Invention and Economic Growth*, Cambridge Mass. (Harvard University Press).

Schumann, P., Prestwood, D., Tong, A. and Vanston, J. (1994), *Innovate!*, New York, (McGraw-Hill).

Schumpeter, J. (1934), *The Theory of Economic Development*, Harvard (Harvard Economic Studies Series, Harvard University) (original German ed. 1911).

Schumpeter, J. (1939), *Business Cycles*, New York (McGraw-Hill).

Schumpeter, J. (1943), *Capitalism, Socialism and Democracy*, London (Unwin).

Schutz, A. (1967), *The Phenomenology of the Social World*, Evanstone Ill. (Heinemann)

Scott, W.R. (1992), *Organizations: Rational, Natural and Open Systems*, Englewood Cliffs (Prentice Hall).

Senge, P. (1995), *The Fifth Discipline. The Art and Practice of the Learning Organization*, London (Century Business)

Sexton, D.L. and Kasarda, J. (eds.) (1992), *The State of the Art of Entrepreneurship*, Boston (PWS-Kent).

Sexton, D.L. and Schön, D.A. (eds.) (1986), *The Art and Science of Entrepreneurship*, Cambridge Mass. (Ballinger).

SIC (Service development, Internationalisation and Competence development) (1999), *Danish Service Firms' Innovation Activities and Use of ICT, Based on a Survey*, Report no. 2, Roskilde (Centre of Service Studies, Roskilde University).

Sjölander, S. (1985), *Management of Innovation*, Göteborg (Department of Industrial Management, Chalmers University of Technology).

Stacey, R.D. (1993), *The Chaos Frontier: Creative Strategic Control for Business*, Oxford (Butterworth-Heinemann).

Stalk, G., Evans, P. and Shulman, L. (1992), Competing on Capabilities: The New Rules of Corporate Strategy, *Harvard Business Review*, vol. 70, pp. 57–69.

Storey, J. (1992), *Developments in the Management of Human Resources*, Oxford (Blackwell).

Strategic Management Journal (1990), Special Issue on Corporate Entrepreneurship, ed. by Schendel, D. and Channon, D., vol. 11, summer.

Sundbo, J. (1991a), Market Development and Production Organization in the Financial Service Firms of the 1990s, *Scandinavian Journal of Management* vol. 7, no. 2, pp. 95–110.

Sundbo, J. (1991b), Strategic Paradigms as a Frame of Explanation of Innovations, *Entrepreneurship and Regional Development*, vol. 3, no. 2 p. 159–73.

Sundbo, J. (1992a), The Tied Entrepreneur, *Creativity and Innovation Management*, vol. 1, no. 3, p. 109–20.

Sundbo, J. (1992b),The Firm as a Dynamic System: Strategic Innovation Management, *Business Annals 1992*, Roskilde (Department of Social Sciences, Roskilde University).

Sundbo, J. (1994), Modulization of Service Production, *Scandinavian Journal of Management*, vol. 10, no. 3, pp. 245–66.

Sundbo, J. (1996), Balancing Empowerment, *Technovation*, vol. 16, no. 8, pp. 397–409.

Sundbo, J. (1997) Management of Innovation in Services, *The Service Industries Journal*, vol. 17, no. 3, pp. 432–55.

Sundbo, J. (1998a), *The Organisation of Innovation in Services*, Copenhagen (Roskilde University Press).

Sundbo, J. (1998b), *The Theory of Innovation – Entrepreneurs, Technology and Strategy*, Cheltenham (Edward Elgar).

Sundbo, J. (1999), Empowerment of Employees in Small and Medium Sized Service Firms, *Employee Relations*, vol. 21, no. 1 and 2, pp. 105–27.

Sundbo, J. and Fuglsang, L. (eds.) (2001), *Innovation as Strategic Reflexivity*, London (Routledge) (forthcoming).

Sundbo, J. and Gallouj, F. (1999), *Innovation in Services – In Seven European Countries*, Centre of Service Studies, Report 99:1, Roskilde (Roskilde University, Centre of Service Studies).

Sundbo, J. and Gallouj, F. (2000), Innovation as a Loosely Coupled System in Services, *International Journal of Services Technology and Management*, vol. 1, no. 1, pp. 15–36.

Tarde, G. (1895), *Les lois de l'imitation*, Paris (Alcan).

Teece, D.J. (1984), 'Economic Analysis and Strategic Management', *California Management Review*, vol. 26, no. 3, pp. 87–110.

Teece, D.J. and Pisano, G. (1994), The Dynamic Capability of Firms: An Introduction, *Industrial and Corporate Change*, vol. 3, no. 3, pp. 537–56.

Teece, D.J., Pisano, G. and Shuen, A. (1997), Dynamic Capabilities and Strategic Management, *Strategic Management Journal*, vol. 18, no. 7, pp. 509–33.

Teece, D.J., Rumelt, R.P., Dosi, G. and Winter, S. (1994), Understanding Corporate Coherence, *Journal of Economic Behavior and Organization*, vol. 23, no. 1, pp. 1–30.

Tidd, J., Bessant, J. and Pavitt, K. (1997), *Managing Innovation*, Chichester (Wiley).

Tushman, M. and Anderson, P. (1997), *Managing Strategic Innovation and Change*, Oxford (Oxford University Press).

Vernon, R. (1966), International Investment and International Trade in the Product Cycle, *Quarterly Journal of Economics*, vol. 80, no. 2, pp. 190–207.

Volberda, H. (1998), *Building the Flexible Firm*, Oxford (Oxford University Press).

Wegloop, P. (1996), Problems and Prospects of Bottom-up Policy Formulation: Towards User-defined Innovation and Technology Policy, *Science and Public Policy*, vol. 23, no. 4, pp. 241–49.

Wernerfelt, B. (1984), A Resource Based View of the Firm, *Strategic Management Journal*, vol. 5, no. 5, pp. 171–80.

Williamson, O.W. (1975), *Markets and Hierarchies*, New York (Free Press)

Winter, S. (1987), Knowledge and Competence as Strategic assets, in Teece, D. (ed.), *The Competitive Challenge*, Cambridge Mass. (Ballinger).

Wood, S. (ed.) (1988), *Continuous Development*, London (Institute of Personnel and Development).

Index